MW01608919

Time in a Bottle Trilogy
Book One
My Brother-in-Law
Got Sick

JOHN HARTIG

Foreword

I took a walk around the block today, Thursday May 9, 2019. I needed to get away from Kenny's Blog, the snippets of which I saved before he passed away, before the whole thing disappeared from the internet.

Kenny died of lung cancer on January 18th, 2008, at the age of 37! Kenny was my brother-in-law, a web designer, a singer, a composer, and an all around computer geek.

He went around in circles within the Niagara medical healthcare system trying to save himself, but he fell victim to waiting times, pills, and with stage 4 lung cancer, eventually he fell victim to that dreaded disease.

He thought the Niagara Healthcare system could have treated him better, and possibly saved his life were he put through to proper channels at reasonable waiting times. He was also critical of the narrow choice the oncologists gave him for treatment. He wanted to try naturopathic medicine, along with traditional methods. He was not impressed with the poor track record of the big 3: chemotherapy, radiation and surgery, i.e. poison, burn and cut.

Kenny launched a foundation called *Voice for Choice*. Now that he is dead, Kenny's foundation has disappeared and his voice against the big pharmaceutical companies and against the slow system has disappeared as well, like his Blog, no longer there, no longer a voice speaking out for change!

On May 26, 2007 Ken wrote, "One of these days I'm gonna take my story public!" This, after receiving a report that he was stage 4 lung cancer, then one week later stage 3 cancer, then later again, stage 4 cancer, as a bureaucratic correction. Since Kenny is no longer with us to take his story public, I'd like to do that for him.

*****

The concept for this *Time in a Bottle Trilogy* grew out of rereading the frustrations Kenny went through during his 10 month battle back in 2007/2008. A battle which he lost. I wanted to give Kenny his voice back. It has been silent for over 10 years, and the system has sadly...not changed.

Money is still being poured into research, which is both a good and a bad thing. It's created a lot of jobs in the field, BUT no cure is found! Kenny said, "There is no money in a cure!"

Cancer took away Kenny's wonderful singing voice and his ability to speak in the later months of his life because cancer damaged his larynx. It also took away his ability to write coherently, so he no longer wrote posts in his Blog; his sister, Marilyn, had to take over. The cancer assassinated his energy so he could no longer fight against what he saw was wrong with the system. He was outraged at the costs of the meds set by pharmaceutical companies and at the billions of dollars which brought no results after decades of fund raising.

This trilogy hopefully gives Ken Janzen his voice back after 10 years of silence.

It's been so long since I looked at what I wrote back in 2007/2008. I kept a diary in those days and copied snippets of *Ken Janzen's*

Health and Wellness Blog over the 10 months he was sick until he died.

Living with leukemia myself since 2003 [a disease which is chronic but stable, thank God] and coping with arthritis, and an aging body at 73 years of age [at the time of this writing], I am determined nevertheless to give Kenny his voice back. A younger version of myself would be more precise in writing, and more up for this fight that Kenny left behind. But I think of David and Goliath, Goliath being "the system".

*****

It is Thursday morning, May 9, 2019. It is 10 a.m. The air outside is fresh, but the trees now have green leaves, the grass is lush and the magnolia blossoms are pink and feel like velvet. This after a miserable, wet and sometimes white winter, where warmth and sunny days seemed like they would never come.

When Ken Janzen died on January 18th, 2008 his personal web sites went off the internet, like little lights going out. Today if you Google his name, the only images and mention of him which pop up, do so because I have made references to him in my own personal web sites.

How easily the trace of any of us disappears from the internet and from the universe itself! Kenny does have a physical headstone though, standing there upright in the back corner of the Vineland Cemetery, which I've visited on a number of occasions. I still wish I were as geeky as he was, and as good on the computer. He was a wonderful web designer.

I thought, if Kenny ever rallied, then he could use the full version of his Blog to write his own book. How we assume that we all will get better if we get sick. I'm glad I kept a diary and copied some snippets from his Blog.

My diary at the time included thoughts on jobs, politics, education, religion and health care and things about my own life from way back, because Kenny's daily posts made me think about those things in my life.

Reading his Blog, one can't but ask oneself: what is the purpose of my own life? How do I fit into this cagey, crazy world of ours? Where is God in all this?

*****

My Trilogy bounces around in time between 2007 and 2012, and beyond. It's a technique not favoured by some writers, but I like it.

When I wrote my diary, I had doubts about its value, and later, even in 2019, I questioned the value about writing this book. Time and time again, I thought about pushing the delete button on my computer. I've heard that the composer, Brahms, burned manuscripts, dissatisfied with the quality of the music, which, I'm sure, was a loss to the world.

I took two significant screen captures when Kenny's Blog was up and running back in 2007 and 2008, **And I Rage** and **The Prodical Son Returns**. Feelings in them sparked a whole stream of thoughts in my diary. I'm glad I made those screen captures as an extra insurance in case Kenny never rallied from his illness, and in case nobody ever saved the Blog. I assumed somebody would surely save the Blog because nobody asked me.

That's why I was grateful that I copied snippets, when I did, and preserved them in a file, aptly named, "Snippets from Kenny's Blog".

Too bad that I didn't save more of Kenny's posts in their entirety. But the family was so busy with grief and doing things for Kenny's kids and wife. My job in the family was to take 5 year old Darriane out for walks when the adults wanted to talk in the kitchen.

I started a Blog of my own back in 2010/2011 after Kenny died, thinking I'd turn that into a book later, but then I scrapped that venture after somebody posted an advertisement in a comment box. There are some pretty ignorant people out there. I continued making entries though in my diary when my personal Blog idea didn't pan out.

I kept questioning the value of what I was doing. Was any of my writing worth it? Would people really be interested in hearing about Kenny's cancer all over again? And read about complaints regarding our broken healthcare system in Canada?

The original idea of healthcare in the days of Tommy Douglas and Lester Pearson back in the 1960s was supposed to be a Universal Healthcare System for all of Canada, one looking after ALL Canadian citizens, care for everybody in this country, rich or poor, a better system than the hodge-podge mess they have in the United States, where all men are supposedly created equal, unless you're a lawyer, an insurance company or a politician!

I wondered whether my personal crusade about Kenny's battle and my own story was worth it, whether this whole literary affair was just "runnin' against the wind", like Bob Seeger says in one of his rock 'n roll songs.

However, this spring day, Thursday morning, May 9, 2019, I decided it was high time to exhume my old diary and those snippets from Kenny's Blog in order to carry on the torch, and like Kenny, continue to rage!

*****

I put publication off a couple of times over the past 10 years. Why? First of all, hesitancy and fear about reopening old wounds, and secondly, cost of publication.

Self-publication is prohibitive because it costs several thousand dollars to get a book into print, and then, the question is, who will read it? Would something about cancer and pain be a real seller? I approached several publishers who rejected the notion outright. So my initial zeal fizzled out, and both my diary and the initial attempt at a book went into hibernation within my computer for several years.

Occasionally I woke the sleeping bear up, and added things to those old files, when an insight hit me now and again. Why not? I was retired. And then I put the pages back to sleep again.

If my computer crashed, I would have nothing to show for all my meticulous work over the years, because pages in a computer are but an arrangement of electrons.

Anyway, when I made entries into my electronic diary, I kept track of the local and global news at the time, so that if there ever was a real reader out there, he or she could see our family's private struggle within the whole context of a world that was often greedy, crazy and stupid back in 2008. Things haven't changed much!

We are but a grain of sand within the entire cosmos. There is nothing new under the sun. I love old clichés, especially when they are true.

John Hartig,
Vineland Author

Synopsis Book One

Book One of the *Time in a Bottle Trilogy* is a book about negotiating the permission from Wally Janzen, Kenny's dad, to write this book. He gave his blessing after much venting about the short-comings in the healthcare system in Niagara, the emails of which I incorporated into Book One. Much of dad's criticism is still true today in 2019, as it was back in 2007.

In 2010, I wrote an initial draft of this book which I considered my "wintery project". I saw the time of *Ken Janzen's Health and Wellness Blog* of 2007/2008 as my home base, a constant Present Time. When I revisited that whole business two years later in 2010 in my attempt at a first draft of the book, I referred to 2010 as going "Back to the Future". Now it is 2019, the time of an actual publication. The concepts get confusing. But flipping back and forth in time doesn't really matter. It's the message that counts.

Lois, a friend from Fair Havens, a Christian Campsite, had some printouts which she had made of Kenny's Blog, back in the summer of 2008. I thought those printouts were a saving grace because nobody thought to save Kenny's Blog after he died.

Well, I shelved those printouts, kept them in a plastic bag for two years, until 2010. Why? I was afraid of revisiting Kenny's pain, and also afraid of discovering that there really wasn't enough material there to feed a book with real substance.

My writing spirit revived in 2010 when I ran across Anwar Knight's Blog on the internet. He wrote about the things he was going through with his own battle of cancer at that time. Anwar is the meteorologist who does the weather report for CTV news in Toronto.

"Ah, another Blog!" I rejoiced, "something like Kenny's! I could compare the two!" Anwar Knight's Blog was a treasure trove of insights, and I started to write again!

Oh yes, before I forget. Kenny was an excellent speller and writer. I decided to keep all his typos and mistakes where he Blogged to show the effects of his meds and the fatigue on his mind when he was battling cancer. So if you come across these errors, they are not Kenny's fault!

I hope this book will be instructive and also stir something of empathy in you.

John Hartig,
Vineland Author

CHAPTER 1

If I Could Save Time

But there never seems to be enough time,
To do the things you want to do
Once you find them...
(Jim Croce 1968)

Post 1:
The First Step in a Painful Journey
Monday, November 15, 2010

MORNING
A sunny day. Tomorrow it will rain. The leaves are raked in the back yard. The laundry is done and hanging outside on the pole. I've got to do the vacuuming before *Peter Gunn* (1960) starts at 12:30 on Retro TV, channel 2-3. That's when I'll eat lunch. A salad, pepperoni stick and toast.

We finally get high-def, digital TV, after a month of experimenting with outdoor acrials to bring in the Buffalo stations from the United States. I don't want to pay for cable or satellite TV. Why pay those companies so much money, when 23 channels are more than enough? Who needs a package of 60 or 100 channels? Who has enough time? Maybe Canadians are more frugal (stingy or wiser?) than Americans.

I'm not supposed to use my wife's name in my writings, but this account of Kenny's Blog and the thoughts in my diary will probably require that, especially since I use the names of my other relatives. Marjorie hates the internet and likes to be anonymous. I can't just call her Anonymous. I can't just say to somebody, "I'd like you to meet my wife, Anonymous." Besides, the name is already used by some guy who writes a lot of poetry and music. I will use the phrase, "my wife", when need be, as a sort of anonymous compromise.

My wife loves NCIS. We finally get 4-1 from Buffalo, so we can watch her favourite crime show at 8 p.m. on Tuesday nights.

Before I rattle on, I forgot to mention the other chore I got done, so my wife doesn't think I just sit on the couch all afternoon watching Audie Murphy westerns.

The eave-troughs are cleaned after an hour of balancing from the roof and scraping rotting leaves out by hand. Ah, the multi-talented tasks of a "house-husband." I never dreamed that this would be my "job description" during retirement.

I'm getting ready for the autumn rains and the winter. The winter! That's when Kenny died, on January 18, 2008, at 37 years of age, lung cancer.

Marjorie and I had his kids over yesterday, on Sunday. It's their periodic visit for Sunday worship service at the Vineland United Mennonite Church, and then lunch (pizza buns) at our house, a visit to Bria, the little dog, at Marjorie's sister's house in the afternoon, and finally depositing the kids back home with their mother Sue in St. Catharines.

It's been almost 3 years since Kenny died. Braeden is 5 now and Darriane is 9. Braeden is in Senior Kindergarten and daddy would be so proud of him. At church, I introduced him as a "senior" and people laughed. Yes, it's been almost 3 years. Daddy would be so proud of Darriane too, his little princess. That's the costume she wore for Halloween in 2005 when they dropped in for "trick or treat".

Next week, the kids are coming again to light a commemorative candle for their daddy at the church. They still remember him. We all need to remember him and not let the door shut on our memories.

This is going to be my wintery project, my snowy day activity, through the next few months to recall things about Ken Janzen's 10 month struggle with lung cancer.

It's a good wintery project when wedding photography goes into hibernation. It'll be therapeutic for me to keep busy pitter-pattering on the computer which will be one way of honouring the memory of Ken Janzen, my dead brother-in-law. I hope that I'm up to the task. I have as yet to unwrap the plastic bag which carries some of the printouts Lois gave me of Kenny's Blog. I've been fearful of opening the contents earlier and looking at those remnants of Kenny's Blog. It's a painful thought to look at the pages.

*****

When I was on the roof, earlier this morning, I joked with the neighbour lady about the fact that I've spent most of my recent weeks, either on the roof or in the crawlspace under our house. I don't know how many times I've been up and down our TV tower at the back of the house or in and out of our crawlspace. My 64 year old bones are achy from positioning and repositioning our TV aerials or running coaxial cables under the floor joists. Thank goodness, my friend Dieter Schuender, another retiree, has given me a helping hand in all this cable and antenna stuff.

I say that the secret to a happy marriage is having two TVs. I intend to get my wife her 32 inch flat screen in the sitting room, so she can watch all the decorating and cooking shows she wants. I intend to run the other line to my own 32 inch TV in the Great Room, so I can watch my sci-fi and my cowboy movies. We do get together for supper though and watch the News on her TV.

Lately I've questioned whether TV watching is worth all this bother. What am I doing lugging and pulling and crawling around at my age? It seems I've always been crawling or digging somewhere throughout my life, whereas other people I've known have skyrocketed into polished careers as professors, doctors or lawyers, professionals who would just pay somebody else to do the grunt-work. But, that's another story...

I suppose I'll be moving back and forth, in my ruminations from Kenny's story to my story just like I've been moving up and down on the house. Like I said, this will be my wintery project, digging through memories while the snow flies.

My job description as "house-husband" is the following: laundry, dishes, suppers and to encourage my wife in her teaching. Some days are so challenging for her, it's a question of survival to the end of the day. There are kids at the school with some real problems, so that teaching stuff from a book is almost beside the point.

My wife is 11 years younger than I am, so she has a number of years to go before retirement, whereas I already crossed that Great Divide.

There's a standing joke between us that "I got myself a young one." But sometimes, neither of us feels that way. We both have health issues and at this rate, neither of us will be ready for the next Olympics!

Marjorie is one of the few dedicated teachers, I know. She lesson plans meticulously and comes home at 6:00 p.m. every night, after getting to the school at 7:30 a.m. My role, therefore, is a different role than the role of the traditional bread winner from the 1950s! Oh how I hated *The Honeymooners*! I wasn't too fond of *I Love Lucy* either.

My brother-in-law, Kenny, was different than me. He was proud of being an entrepreneur, having his own web design company, being successful at it and being the bread-winner in his family. He was also a good presenter and salesman for companies to sign up with him for new web designs because he knew what he was talking about. He knew his business.

When he was stricken with lung cancer, all that go-get-um entrepreneurial spirit and independence disappeared, and within months, he was couch confined. I can't imagine the mental anguish he must have gone through thinking about where the money was coming from to support his family, and where to look for medical help for his cancer. Kenny created a Blog, in March 2007, so he could talk about his battle: *Ken Janzen's Health & Wellness Blog*.

My intention, after 3 years since Kenny died, is to write a book about Kenny's experience and also my own questions about career and life, with the hope that there are some things that people can identify with and maybe learn from.

When Kenny started his Wellness Blog, he made no bones about it being "his" Blog and that he was the master of the content, especially the length of any comments submitted to it. There were so many teeny one or two liners that came in which were nice but which were repetitive and which (I felt) added no literary value to what might eventually become a book.

Kenny, I think, harboured the thought that, once his illness was cured, his Blog might indeed be crafted into a book, but that never happened.

My contributions during the existence of the Wellness Blog got longer and longer, as Kenny got sicker and sicker. I always have something to say, ask anybody! Especially when it comes to writing. I hoped my comments were filled with significant insights, so that Kenny would eventually have something worthy for publication. Perhaps I overestimated my skill in being the white knight of good writing. I don't know.

Well, that notion that long, philosophical comments were good was shot down by Kenny. He didn't see it that way. There was another contributor, as well, who was gently castigated for making his comments too long and too rambling. In short order, we drew in our horns and made our comments shorter, and stayed more in line of what other people had to say. Soon, I withdrew making comments altogether in the Blog and Kenny noticed that.

But before I ramble on too much about things far ahead, I'd like to say something about Kenny's Web Design business. Kenny ran his web design business from the basement of his house and he was often the cook and bottle washer there too, though meals, I understand, were somewhat erratic at the home because of the demands of his self-employed profession. His basement was where his computers and musical instruments were, where he produced his superb web designs, and where he recorded the songs he composed himself. That was his domain where he worked at all hours of the day or night.

CHAPTER 2

Monday, November 15, 2010

A few weeks after Kenny died, his personal web sites disappeared from the internet. As I said before, like lights going out one by one, since the payments were not made to his server for renewals.

I got some screen captures of his Blog and of his personal sites, before they all disappeared. I incorporated those screen captures later on in his dad's site, Blumengarten.org. This preserved a semblance of Kenny's excellent work of what he had in his kenjanzen.com site, as well as what he had in the sites he created for his two little kids, Braeden and Darriane.

I managed dad's site for a bunch of years with the links that led to Kenny's old pages of what he did as a web site artist. But I know, as dad gets older too, and has little use for the computer, dad's personal website will disappear, and in fact, it has since he sold Blumengarten and downsized to a smaller house in Fonthill. As people downsize, I am always reminded that we are all but dust in the wind.

I wish I had half Kenny's talent in design and one quarter of his technical scripting skill. After he died, his virtual reality died too. There was no proof of his existence anymore, no sign of him on the internet. His personal web sites were wiped out. Google could not find him. I brought his presence back by writing about him in my own personal website, johnhartig.ca Google found him there.

AFTERNOON

So here I've started my memoir of Ken Janzen's Battle on this day, November 15, 2010.

I hope it will be preserved in some way and not disappear in the "Ethernet" like Kenny's Blog did. I launched my writing today as a Blog in Wordpress, since Kenny chose that service in which to keep track of his illness way back in 2007 where he could record his thoughts about his illness with lung cancer.

Unless someone else did it that I don't know about, it's too bad we couldn't save all of Kenny's posts. At the time though, the family wasn't thinking about saving "the writing" while the actual man was in the process of dying.

I wasn't sure I wanted to write about this at all. I do not wish to touch on the nerves of various family members, but I figure what Kenny went through in his sickness and in the medical profession which treated that sickness, all that should not be forgotten! As a writer, I also want to have my say!

I know that much of Canada is turned off by the mention of church now-a-days but I hope that people will understand that this is an integral part of the Janzen family life, especially since their heritage is Mennonite. So I will mention Faith and God on occasion in my writings.

To recap: My brother-in-law, Ken Janzen, died on January 18, 2008 at 3:39 pm. He lost a 10 month battle against lung cancer. Ken was 37 years old and left a young family behind: his wife, Sue, and his two wonderful children, Darriane 6 at the time, and Braeden 2.

I was privileged to have Ken Janzen as my brother in law. He was also survived by his father, Wally Janzen, and his two sisters, Marilyn, Jerry Schroeder's wife, and Marjorie, my wife.

*****

In April 2007, Ken and Sue Janzen had their lives and that of their family unexpectedly changed forever. Ken was diagnosed with "*poorly differentiated non-small cell adenocarcinoma*" in his lungs (one of the more aggressive forms of lung cancer). His official 'prognosis' was approximately 6 months, possibly 12 months with chemotherapy and radiation.

Ken could no longer work as a graphic/web designer and things became financially challenging since he was self-employed. Family and friends pitched in to give a helping hand at a fundraiser held at the Beamsville Secondary School on Sunday, June 24, 2007. The fundraiser was also made possible through donations from numerous businesses who showed a sense of generous corporate responsibility.

Ken combined this fundraiser with the release of his debut CD, *My Sentiments Exactly*, calling this gala affair not just a fundraiser but his CD Release Party! Over 600 people dropped in throughout the day. He celebrated his 37th birthday on August 5, 2007. He was still healthy enough in the early autumn months to go to his daughter's soccer games.

Kenny hoped for a cure.

He proposed a foundation, *Voice for Choice*, which championed alternative medicines and treatments to give people choices other than the 3 traditional paths of chemotherapy, radiation and surgery for cancer patients. Kenny created an internet diary, a

20

Blog, which thousands of people read and commented on from all over the world.

Ken Janzen's Health and Wellness Blog is an open and honest journey through his thoughts and his medical status as he battled his cancer. It's a learning experience for all of us, to become better people, to be givers and not takers in this world.

The Blog opens in March 2007 with titles like: **CT Scans and Surgeons - Oh My!** and **The Saga Continues**. The title for April 27, 2007 was: **And I Rage!**

With Kenny's knack for words, his passion for a decent medical system, his frustrations and humanity, the writings in his Blog have the makings of an excellent book which upon reading could make us all better human beings. The last entry of Kenny's Blog was on January 25, 2008, put in by Kenny's sister, Marilyn. It was Kenny's **Eulogy**. Kenny's **www.thejanzenfamily.com/Blog** no longer exists (except for the 2 pages I managed to get a screen capture of and insert into dad's web site, blumengarten.org, which now in 2019 also no longer exists.

CHAPTER 3

Monday, November 15, 2010
EVENING:
My wife came home tonight at her usual 6:00 p.m. She gets to school at 7:45 a.m. and leaves at 5:45 p.m. I've told her often enough that I'd support her in becoming a principal but she says, "Too many bureaucratic hassles!" She'd make a great principal with her brain for organization, intelligence, her calmness and wisdom.

Anyway, the hamburgers were barbecued by 6:15 p.m. and supper was ready. She took out her Lee Child murder mystery, *Gone Tomorrow*. She ate and read, while I ate and watched *The Incredible Hulk* (1983) on Retro TV, channel 2-3.

It was an episode about a company that polluted the town's water system. The CEO lied that the water system in the town was polluted from an overabundance of chlorine, whereas it was really E coli. A female employee attempted to retrieve "progress reports" which proved the deception.

"Ha!" my wife piped up, "progress reports...I had to spend 2 hours per kid!" She had tuned in to that specific reference because we had just put in 47 hours total in the last two weeks, evenings and weekends, coming up with comments for the "new and improved" report cards that were supposed to replace the formulaic jargon in the old report card system, formerly used by her school board. My wife also added how her NeoCitron drink tasted worse than the stuff *The Incredible Hulk* had to deal with in the polluted water system.

She did not fall in love with the taste of this "natural remedy" to help her sinus allergies. "Get me a handful of almonds please, and some juice," she asked. "Maybe that'll make my sore throat feel better. I eat and I drain!"

It's not fair that she inherited all these gluten sensitivities. I can think of some really unworthy people who should have these problems instead.

"You're not living up to your potential," I said. "If you were healthy, you'd be so much more energetic and perky. I know how you could be or should be," I continued. "I hope we sleep tonight."

Bill Bixby, by the way, who starred in *The Incredible Hulk*, died of prostrate cancer in 1993. And so it goes!

What are the food companies in North America doing to us anyway with all those preservatives and additives? Or has cancer always been so rampant and our forefathers just didn't know what they died from?

I've accepted my wife's allergies. It's "our" problem, not just hers, and we accept each other in all these things. Love and loyalty is so different than the pabulum fed to us by Hollywood in those romance movies.

My wife has seen me through a nervous breakdown when the going was tough. Couples have thrown in the towel a lot sooner and for a lot less during stressful times, when the divorce rate is over 50%, when both partners have to work or have careers, when kids have become "latchkey kids," lacking real parents and wise role models at home. I'm glad to have her to spend the rest of my life with. How did she ever find me in Grande Prairie, Alberta, where I felt like a speck of sand tossed on an endless sea, trying to find my compass and a purpose. Well, we live with what we've got and we do our best.

CHAPTER 4

Post 2:
Unsung Heroes, All of Us!

We are all unsung heroes, each one of us with our own private story, that is played out bravely and quietly and never told. And so it goes! But why not sing of this? Why not tell Kenny's story or mine? We all have our unsung bravery and our own unspoken story!

Thank goodness, I learned how to write, so many years ago, as a news reporter for a small town paper in Grande Prairie, Alberta, *The Booster*. Ah, the good old days, at minimum wages and 60 hours per week. But that's another story in itself...maybe that was part of Kenny's story too, because he worked huge hours per week at his graphics and design job, truly absorbed in his work at all hours.

Kenny and I were a generation apart. He was 24 years younger than I. I liked to think of myself as belonging more to his generation because I liked most of the same rock music and many of the same action films. Plus I had a keen interest in web design.

I always gravitated towards younger tastes and knew the names of so many of the young singers. I couldn't play guitar or sing like Kenny, so I was just the "hip" older brother-in-law on the outskirts of his circle of friends. I didn't mind though. When I was in his company, I still felt like I was young at heart, and I was accepted.

Let's see? Kenny was born on August 5, 1970. That makes him a Leo on the Zodiac. Traditional positive traits for Leos are: generous, warmhearted, creative, enthusiastic, broad-minded, expansive, faithful and loving. He was all of those! Whenever the family had a computer glitch, he was there, click, click, clicking until the thing was fixed. He'd show up with a Timmy's coffee in hand. Creative? We cherish his three drawings in our Great Room. Enthusiastic? He'd get excited over a new web design, "look at this effect or that effect"! Kenny doted on his two kids and loved his wife immensely. Darriane was his little princess and Braeden was his little "pucker-boy".

Now, the Zodiac also says that Leos have a dark side: pompous, patronizing, bossy, interfering, dogmatic and intolerant. I can see some of that in Kenny but you can't brush a person over with one large stroke. Kenny was a complicated mixture of a personality. He knew he was talented and reveled in it. Enjoyed it. Showed it. But I've never seen him being pompous about it. Mind you, he could be bossy. He had to be definite and speak his own mind. After all, he ran his own business! He also was dogmatic about his beliefs in what was right or wrong. Intolerant? Maybe sometimes. He couldn't stand arrogance and lies in other people, especially in business practices, because he drove to the heart of the matter, tried to get at the nuts and bolts of things, and he liked to deliver the goods in a well-done web design product.

He was a master craftsman in design, creating attractive web sites for his clients, many of whom became personal friends, like Jim Gardner from Toronto who owned the Brüzer clothing company. Clients gravitated towards him because of Kenny's work ethic, his honesty and his computer know-how.

I've often thought that, had Kenny taken me underwing as a protégé in web design, it might not have worked out. His mind was too quick and I doubt if he had the patience to slow down for someone who was a plodder like me. I just didn't quite get things the first time.

I went to night school at Mohawk College instead to learn web design the slow "academic way". Kenny picked things up on his own with the speed of a click. I don't know how he did it. He also had a tendency, to do everything himself to get it done just right. There'd be a starburst of energy and he'd attack a project with the speed of light.

Yet, I'm sure when Kenny taught his dad how to do email, he would slow down to dad's pace and make sure dad picked up how to do it.

"The Leo type is the most dominant, spontaneously creative and extrovert of all the zodiacal characters. In grandeur of manner, splendor of bearing and magnanimity of personality, they are the monarchs among humans as the lion is the king of beasts." **(search.conduit.com)**

I don't "believe" in Zodiac signs. But this little exercise served well to talk about Kenny. Zodiac signs are a great amusement, if you're fingering one of those place mats at a restaurant. If you're scratching your head about what to say about a person's character though, I guess googling traits for Leos comes in handy too, as a conversation starter. Happily, most of the characteristics listed for Leos applied spot on to my brother-in-law. He was a unique guy, a Lion among men!

Hmmm? Actually I see him more like a Tiger, not a Lion! Tigers are more colourful, fierce survivors and mostly larger than lions. Kenny could be larger than life and he was blessed with a fierceness to survive. He fought fiercely for life and hung on tenaciously even to the last of his last 10 months of life. Had he survived, he would have come back even bigger and stronger:

> *Risin up -- back on the street,*
> *Did my time, took my chances*
> *Went the distance now I'm back on my feet*
> *Just a man and his will to survive --*
> *So many times, it happens too fast,*
> *You trade your passion for glory,*
> *Don't lose your grip on the dreams of the past,*
> *You must fight just to keep them alive*
>
> **its the eye of the tiger,*
> *Its the thrill of the fight,*
> *Rising up to the challenge of our rival,*
> **(Survivor "Eye of the Tiger" 1982)**

CHAPTER 5

Post 3:
What doesn't kill you

My wife and I have often talked about survival amidst all the things that life throws at you unexpectedly. However, we both take that Nietzsche statement with a grain of salt: "What doesn't kill you, makes you stronger!"

It may be true for those people who have enough health and stamina to begin with, but for many people, the reality is that some problems like cancer can just plain exhaust you and at the end, will kill you. Certainly, if you survive you can appreciate life in a renewed vigorous way. But if you're too sick and worn down like Kenny was, well, you die. Even Superman can succumb to Kryptonite.

Friedrich Nietzsche (d. 1900) apparently looked at life in black and white terms. You either get stronger or you die.

Maybe his intelligence made him superior, the intolerant "übermensch." There was no middle ground in his philosophy and no understanding. But I think most people fall in the middle within the normal curve of life's experiences.

Sure, often the top rung of Supermen become stronger to face even bigger challenges. All the more power to them! The bottom rung falls victim and dies when trials and tribulations are just too big. Then there's most of us where trials and tribulations are not big enough to kill...but they sure wear you down.

I'm thinking of lives depicted in the *Germinal* novel by Emile Zola, the French author, who wrote about the terrible living conditions of 19th century coalminers who suffered at the hands of "les Gras", the fat, rich bosses of society.

Maybe Nietzsche might have thought poor people deserved their fate because they didn't have the ability to rise above it all. But he was a university professor living in a comfortable shell of academia with his head in the theoretical clouds of philosophy. Even in today's society, if a person is beset with health issues year after year, a person can just lead an existence and not really live life, being so worn down. Nietzsche should have learned that lesson in his day because he resigned from the University of Basel in 1879, at the age of 35, due to health reasons and at a later date in 1889, he became mentally ill (probably from syphilis). Perhaps, in the short term, Nietzsche saw himself as becoming stronger overcoming his setbacks but in the long term, he was just enduring existence himself.

In the 21st century, we now hear a lot about verbal abuse by a boss in the work place. An employee's self-esteem gets worn down, where you come to the point of just enduring a job in a weakened state, which doesn't necessarily make you a stronger person, just a submissive one.

Yet it's amazing how indomitable the human spirit can be though, despite all odds. Yes, there is truth in Nietzsche's philosophy (I don't dispute that completely, that you get stronger and wiser with trials). Kenny and his business partner (and friend), Frank Pizzacalla, must have faced a lot of ups and downs in making their *Effectiv Design* company finally succeed. You fail in something, you readjust and then try again.

I came into their little office in St. Catharines one day, about when they started back in 2000, and saw them figuring out scripting for a link on a web page. It looked like gobbledygook to me at the time. "Fascinating," I thought.

Kenny scanned a bunch of my photographs for a web site he was building for *Peninsula Tourism*. So he and Frank not only had to learn the mechanics of their trade on the job (often as they were doing it) but also had to go out and be confident salesmen to draw in more clients for their growing business.

The ups and downs in their business made them stronger entrepreneurs, and within 2 years, made their company quite attractive for a buy-out in the web design industry in Niagara. Kenny and Frank got enough capital from their successful venture with *Effectiv Design* to pursue separate careers.

Kenny went on to work as Creative Director for *Target Internet Development* between 2002 and 2004. I'm sure, he and the company he worked for, must have faced similar ups and downs there, because that's what businesses do in a competitive market.

Kenny was a quick study. I can see him soaking up a lot more business smarts which made him shrewder and, in fact, be a better survivor in the growing web design market.

He went out on his own again in 2004/05 to create *MoreStyle*, which became another highly competitive web design company, reaching beyond Niagara into the Toronto markets. He won an award in Niagara for a best design.

Kenny had a knack for picking himself up, dusting himself off and starting all over again!

> *Sometimes you have to fall*
> *To find out who you are*
> *Don't be afraid to fail*
> *Because you learn each time you try*
> *Sometimes you have to fall...to fly*
>   **(Oakridge Boys "Fall To Fly" 2001)**

Kenny did not need a Nietzsche to tell him that challenges make you stronger. It's just that, there are times, when things in life are just plain insurmountable. He could handle things that came from the outside business world, but when the enemy came from inside his own body, like lung cancer, that was a different story! And that's what Kenny had to face in the end. But even then, he was becoming, not necessarily a stronger man, but a better man.

CHAPTER 6

Post4:
Emails between Dad and Me
Saturday, November 13, 2010
From Wally [Dad]:

Hi John:

I have been reading Ty Bollinger's book, "Cancer - Step Outside the Box," a well-written book detailing how seven members of his immediate family all died of cancer. When his mom died, he felt that he needed to do some research into looking for answers to what the conventional medical community does to "cure" cancer.

What he discovered shocked him as it might you. He doesn't mince any words in what the FDA (Food and Drug Association), the AMA (American Medical Association) and the ACS (American Cancer Society) have done to keep any and all alternative cancer treatments from the American people in order that the big pharmaceutical companies may continue selling their nauseatingly expensive chemotherapy drugs and make money for their shareholders.

As I have heard and read so many times before: It's all about the money! It's NOT really about trying to cure people.

In his book, Mr. Bollinger includes an allegory written by Mike Adams, editor of Natural News, known as the Health Ranger, called, "Welcome to the Town of Allopath" to give the readers an idea how insane the conventional healthcare industry in the U.S. and Canada has become. It is well worth reading.

You can read it by going here:

www.naturalnews.com/008674.html

(Wally)

_____

Tuesday, November 16, 2010

Hi Dad:

I'm writing a book, some of it on Kenny. I would like your permission to proceed. I want to take what we salvaged from Kenny's Blog, and mix it together with things that happened in my life.

I'm not at the stage where I've decided to launch the book, until I get a lot of preliminary writing done. If I use any of Kenny's Blog, it will be a difficult chore because there were so many comments in it which were short and scattered. There were also so many things repeated, that strict editing is required. I would like to use only the comments with some length and substance. Even with that I'm not sure if Kenny's Blog can be turned into an actual book that the general public might find interesting. Then there is the problem of finding a publisher and paying for that.

Anyway, I want you to be the editor and proof-reader in the preliminary stages of such a book. Of course, the whole thing may fizzle out, if we don't find a publisher. This will keep me busy through most of the winter, until wedding photography picks up again next spring. I also want to emphasize that this is my project now, under my direction with whatever writing skills I have. I'm looking for direction and valuable insight from family as I plug along, but the end product will be my doing. I don't want to feel handcuffed.

I want to talk about Kenny's last 10 months of life (basically the lifespan of his Blog) but with offshoots to my own reflections, life experiences and opinions. I think a double thread will make it a stronger written project. But I guess I'm asking for your permission and blessing on this first. I know this may open old wounds but I think Kenny's story needs telling in some form.

John

_____

Tuesday, November 16, 2010

Hi John,

I have been struggling with getting myself primed to continue writing material about Kenneth, especially his years after he left home where he tried to fend for himself, but I just can't bring myself to do it. It is like you said, I will, I know, merely reopen wounds that haven't even thought about healing, yet. So it is with profound relief to hear that you are willing to continue his story.

I have several chapters of his early life which I would be more than happy to send to you, if you want to do a biography on him.

Had Kenneth lived, managed to recover from his cancer, he was determined to demand that all cancer patients be allowed to choose which healing pattern they wished to follow rather than be subjected to the "Big 3" i.e. chemo, surgery, and radiation. If you recall, he was going to title it, "Voice for Choice." He already knew that what the cancer industry provided to all cancer patients covered by the Canada Health Plan was about as useless in curing cancer as doing nothing. He knew that the cancer industry was almost the sole cause of our Health Care being in such dire straits regarding finances.

When Marilyn wrote Kenneth's obituary, she requested that NO donations in his memory be given to the Cancer Society. That would have been entirely in keeping with his wishes.

I would hope that your "story" would include much of his thoughts regarding the corrupt cancer industry enabled by an equally corrupt bureaucracy (our government). Although I have come across many books about this very thing since his death, Kenneth was well aware of the greed in the pharmaceutical industry that was the power house behind the cancer industry.

I would be most happy to have you read these books BEFORE you embark on your "mission".

Wally

CHAPTER 7

Post4 cont'd:
Emails between Dad and Me

Hi Dad:

What you want to create is a biography of Kenneth. That is different than my goal in my story. A biography is a separate genre, more suitable to completing after and if my thing ever gets published. I want to focus on what we salvaged from Kenny's Blog (from the print-outs that Lois at Fair Havens gave us) with reflections about how Kenny's posts relate to my own thoughts about life, belief in God, and the medical profession.

My Blog will turn out to be as much of Kenny in there, as of me. That is way different than a straight biography and your thoughts on Kenny's life. We are talking about two different potential books here.

I think you could use what I produce as an inspiration and launching pad to finish your biography of Kenneth at a later date. If my thing gets published, then your efforts may stand a better chance of being published anyway.

I'll help you at that stage if you want and I'll even read some of the literature on the cancer profession you suggested. I'm sure you have a lot to say about the medical profession and the pharmaceutical companies and could go into more detail than I could or even want to at this stage in my writing. Your goal needs a separate book, which would do justice to your own memories and to your justified venting. Let's look at this as a one two punch about the mishandled cancer care system in both the United States and in Canada. My novel and your biography!

When you are ready I will give you a link to the book I am writing this winter.

I thought originally of creating a Blog for my thoughts, like Kenny did using the online Wordpress company, same colour scheme and all, but then as I write my venture is becoming more like a publishable book.

John

Dear Dad:

It's clearer now what I'd like to do in my writing. I want to use Kenny's posts and melt them into my own thoughts and meanderings, as I see fit. Instead of a full biography, I want to concentrate on Kenny's last 10 months of life, basically the life of his Blog. Recalling incidences about him, during that time, are important.

I remember very significantly how our boy reacted when he heard that crash downstairs when the cabinet fell and Darriane was in the basement...when he broke his toe rushing around the corner to see if his little girl was hurt. I want to include all those things from what I remember him doing and from his talks with family. I don't know if you can handle this Wally or want me to contact you as I go along.

The other concern I have, Wally, is that I remain in control of what goes into my story and how it's done.

I don't want anyone "taking over" and putting pressure on me to change this or that, so it's no longer recognizably my work. How do I balance this request out with family and still remain the captain of my ship?

There can be several books coming out of Kenny's experience, including his biography.

I hate to see things fizzle out, either because people are too busy to remember him or because they want to say too much their own way. Yes, there is so much of my own past life I'd like to include in this story but also of present times, like Darriane lighting a candle on Sunday in commemoration of her daddy.

I'm not sure where I'm going with this, except that I don't want to come into a no-contact zone with you and the family because of the memory and the pain. I also don't want to have my story turn into a platform simply for diatribing about the pharmaceuticals and the health system because that also is another book in itself.

As to the health system and the pharmaceuticals, I'd like to include that where appropriate and where Kenny talks about them. I'm sure there will be lots of room in my writing for that with your input.

I will not exclude the problems in our health system, they need to be mentioned. I want to mention how Kenny was treated at the hospitals, the doctors he encountered, the refusal to sign for his morphine and the painful trip to the Juravinski Clinic in Hamilton (which involved his sisters, Marilyn and Marjorie).

I want to describe the fundraiser and how that money disappeared like water for buying meds at the family's own expense and then the funeral. There is so much in the immediate past that needs dealing with, so that a biography would be too massive to include at this stage. Also, it being my own writing, I deliberately want it to have my experiences in life and my reflections interjected as an author.

How do we do this? Or do we let it fizzle out because there are too many people who have things to say and too many angles involved? I also want to make sure there are no obvious lawsuits and family feuds created out of this gargantuan venture.

Love ya dad,
John

CHAPTER 8

Post 5:
Short changing Cancer Patients
Wednesday, November 17, 2010

Hi John:

Go right ahead. But please, as you post and talk about his reactions and comments etc., please include, if at all possible how the cancer industry short changes all cancer patients, especially Kenneth, who chose not to go the chemo route, even though the oncologist told him that he might possibly gain 3 more months of life.

She told him that without their intervention, the best he could expect was six months. Yet he lived almost an entire year after diagnosis.

Was he ever offered hydrazine sulphate which most likely would have stopped the cachexia (wasting away) cold? Or was he given Cesium Chloride which might well have given him additional years? Or protocell? No, he was offered chemotherapy because that's where the money is. (It is said that for every cancer patient, the cancer industry stands to gain upwards of half a million dollars.) There are so MANY non-toxic treatments that have a MUCH BETTER track record than anything the cancer industry has to offer, but they are all extremely inexpensive and there is no money to be made from these. The public needs to know about this. According to all reports, chemo has a cure rate of approximately 3%, yes, only three percent whereas other alternative treatments have a cure rate for stage four cancer cases close to 50%.

We should never have lost our boy. You can be sure that the oncologists know all too well about these alternative treatments but if they were to use them, or even suggest them, they might well lose their licenses.

We have a CORRUPT health care industry all controlled by the pharmaceutical industry and the government (read: bureaucrats).

Wally

Wednesday, November 17, 2010
Noon
Dear Dad:
I've written two pages of a potential book and am on the verge of typing up Kenny's posts, one by one, from the printouts that Lois gave us. But I haven't touched them yet!

I haven't had the courage to take them out of the plastic bag and see what's in there. It will be a huge job to retype everything into the computer. If it were not for Lois, we would basically have nothing of Kenny's Blog because none of us thought of saving anything from the internet because we were all grieving.

If my book gets published, Kenny's posts will at least be in print for the public to read. I have to put Kenny's posts in order and then determine what to say about each one of them and also decide if and when I should expose my book to family members.

I'm sort of presuming that Lois saved some of the more significant posts that Kenny actually wrote. I know Marilyn took over for him closer to Christmas time when he could no longer think straight and have the energy to do things himself. So what's in Lois' printouts is all based on speculation and hope.

I don't want to include too much of what was in the comment boxes in the Blog. Although those comments were nice, they were short and they didn't have any of, what I call, real literary substance.

I'm well aware how superficial the social networks are, like *Twitter* and *Facebook*, and I want to shy away from that kind of trivia.

Kenny thought *Facebook* was a great idea but I feel it takes away from reality and gobbles up people's valuable time. The other thing which crossed my mind is that, if I do invite family to say things in my book, before I know it, I may have family feuds on my hands. As a Jewish friend once said about his own family, Oiveee.

It should be noted here too that the comment boxes in a Blog are susceptible to hackers, like what happened to Kenny's Blog in the summer of 2007 where, all of a sudden, thousands of links to porno sites poured in. What a pernicious thing to do, how perverse! That alone was a huge task in itself to delete that garbage, and then to keep these hurtful intrusions out of the Blog from day to day.

Well, I've stirred the waters, and I'm so close to taking the plunge in resuscitating some of what Kenny said. Blogs are not my thing, but some kind of writing has to be done which will make people aware of what Kenny suffered in his last 10 months, even if it's not a Blog.

An actual book is sounding more and more appealing.

John

CHAPTER 9

The Love Song of J. Alfred Prufrock
T.S. Eliot June 1915

And indeed there will be time
To wonder, "Do I dare?" and, "Do I dare?"
Time to turn back and descend the stair,
With a bald spot in the middle of my hair-

I haven't looked at the print-outs yet that Lois at Fair Havens provided for us, what was it? – two summers ago. I don't even know her last name but I'm grateful to her. It's been almost 3 years since Kenny's death and I still haven't taken those print-outs out of the plastic bag to take a peek.

Of all the people who visited the Blog, it seems Lois was the only one who took the time to print some pages out of Kenny's Blog because she thought they really said something.

We were fortunate to get a remnant of the Blog from her. I've still got the family photo albums in the corner of my study which Sue gave back to us. What do we do with those old pictures? I've been meaning to scan a lot of the childhood photos of Kenny but that's very time consuming, and it seems, I can never find the time in my own life to do this.

I've tucked all of Lois's print-outs into a corner of my cabinet and shied away from looking at them, mainly because of fear. It's hard to relive the difficult 10 months before Kenny's death and what fluctuating emotions he expressed in his posts. Poring over the intelligent journal of someone recording his own death, clinging on to a hope of some salvation despite everything, is scary.

I can appreciate how stymied you feel, dad, in continuing to write a biography on Kenneth. Too many memories, too much pain! Maybe there will never be enough time to heal this wound...and we're not getting any younger! Reminds me of Hamlet saying to Polonius: "for yourself, sir, shall grow old as I am, if like a crab you could walk backward." Or in the movie, *The Curious Case of Benjamin Button*, where he grows backward in age: "Life can only be understood looking backward. It must be lived forward."

By looking back at Kenny's life, we are trying to make sense of why he died so young and to understand his mind as he suffered in his journey but it is difficult to just stop our own lives to do this.

> But at my back I always hear
> Time's winged chariot hurrying near;
> And yonder all before us lie
> Deserts of vast eternity.
>   Andrew Marvell (d. 1678)

When the clocks get turned back in autumn, one hour, too bad we can't turn them back 3 years, so we could catch Kenny's cancer in time to cure him. Now that our own lives continue to move forward, it's scary looking backward, so the old photo albums rest in the corner untouched, and the print-outs from the Blog don't get looked at. I'm hoping to get enough gumption to look at the print-outs next week. It's about time! I just don't know where to start.

Like time's winged chariot, I feel more of an urgency now to get down to it, especially with winter approaching when time will lie more heavily on my hands. If I were 30 years younger and not 64, I'd have a job to go to and I certainly wouldn't have the time to fill up blank pages with memories. Those memories would be tucked away in a place where they don't hurt.

But I do feel more a sense of urgency to get something down in print, now that I'm 64 and "unemployed". Keeping my mind focused and my writing on the task at hand will be tough! I have a tendency to get sidetracked a lot when things come to me unbidden and unasked out of the blue:

> *Will you still need me, will you still feed me,*
> *When I'm sixty-four.*
>
> *You'll be older too,*
> *And if you say the word,*
> *I could stay with you.*
> (The Beatles – 1967)

CHAPTER 10

Post 6:
Two Months later
End of January 2011

Friday, January 28, 2011
3:13 p.m.

Hi Dad:

Whew!! I've retyped all the posts that Lois at Fair Havens gave us.

I will preserve the Blog/post format in the first several chapters of my book because that's how I started my writing but later on, I intend to switch over into a straight book format with which I feel more comfortable. I intend to delete my Wordpress Blog.

Those posts that we got from Lois are basically the ones from Kenny's last few months, going from October 2007 to January 2008 when he died. I was disappointed in their content. I was hoping for Kenny's earlier posts in spring and summer. There will be less of him to work with since he gave up Blogging in December and then Marilyn took over.

But what I've typed into the computer will have to do. It's been a mammoth and painful task retyping some of Kenny's posts, and reading them as I go. I can understand if family just wants to forget the whole business, and say, delete it, don't write any of it!

I'm expanding my book beyond Kenny, to discuss religion, current events and my daily activities because a lot of this originates from my own diary. My ponderings and Kenny's posts are so intertwined. Even if family asked me to do it, I would not delete any of Kenny's entries because a lot of my thoughts go hand in hand. There should be no objection to what I am doing. The story needs to be told.

I'm sort of wondering though, if I should go ahead and seek out a publisher now, before I inform any of the family, just so that we have a company already in place who is willing to print this thing. Ironically, with all the hard work ahead, there still may be nothing that comes of this.

I can forward to you Wally the chapter that I've written thus far entitled "Kenny's Blog and Lung Cancer". I can understand if you don't want it.

Love Ya,
John

Friday, January 28, 2011
3:37 p.m.

Hi John,
Yes I would appreciate a copy of that special chapter.
Thanks in advance.
Wally

Tuesday, February 1, 2011
5:06 p.m.

Dear Wally:

I've got one and a half chapters to go in what looks like a 12 chapter book. I don't know if you want any other chapters forwarded to you. The one I sent you, Chapter 4, in the first draft of my book, tells about Kenny's 10 month battle. It included things from his website about his work philosophy, his merry-go-round experience within the medical system, and his sleepless nights. It was a very difficult to write chapter.

So if you're interested in any of the other chapters, I can forward them to you as well, as I finish and polish things a bit more in my drafts.

John

_____

Tuesday, February 1, 2011
9:17 p.m.

Hi John,

I'm still digesting what you sent me about Kenneth. I am able to read only so much at a time. In fact, for the last two nights Kenneth has figured greatly in my dreams.

How I wish he were still with us.

Since his death I have been reading so much about cancer and how to treat it and the more I read the angrier I get.

Why is our CMA (Canadian Medical Association) and the FDA (Food and Drug Administration in the US) so insistent on doing whatever they can to suppress any and all alternative treatments for cancer when they KNOW that chemo has a track record of only two to three percent cure rate. And it bothers me to think of the many cancer patients who will be sacrificed on the altar of greed. For every cancer patient it is determined that the health care industry (that's oncologists, family doctors, hospitals, pain management doctors, pharmaceutical companies) stands to gain more than half a million dollars before the patient dies. How much money will they make if the patient is cured????

Alternative Cancer clinics are still being raided in the U.S. and are not allowed in Canada. I believe there are something like 13 or 14 rather good cancer clinics in Mexico where you will find all the Hollywood crowd who contract cancer. Even Ronald Reagan went to Germany to have his colon cancer treated with hyperthermia. These Mexican clinics use hyperthermia as well as insulin potentiating therapy and building up the patient's immunity so his body can fight the rogue cancer cells. Chemo, on the other hand, destroys the patient's immunity. How could our doctors get it so wrong!!!!!
Kenneth was told by his oncologist that proper nutrition played NO role in cancer. Yet ALL alternative doctors say that because of our poor nutrition, the body is ripe for cancer cells to develop.

And I could go on and on.
Please keep your other chapters for the time being. Thanks.

Wally

CHAPTER 11

Monday, February 7, 2011
11:19 a.m.

Dear Wally:

I know now how my book will end, with my birthday, which will be on February 23, 2011, in about two weeks when I will turn 65. Normally, that's retirement age. Kenny would be 40 at that time had he lived. Difficult to think of him other than in his 20s or 30s!

The book is already at a decent length and covers all the topics I wish to write about.

Originally, I'd started it as a Blog and then when I got an unsolicited comment, I took my Blog offline and began refashioning it into a straight book format. I sure didn't want that same terrible experience we all had with Kenny's Blog where porn links were dumped into the comment boxes. What a shameful crime that was!

I've included all the remnants salvaged from *Ken Janzen's Health & Wellness Blog* of 2007-2008. I've also structured much of my book in diary format, mixed with current events and some of my daily experiences in 2010 and 2011. I've included my commentaries as I went along and much of my own history.

I'm hoping that the book will not be dated in a year or two and become irrelevant. Kenny's suffering and our losing him should have a "timeless application", for other families in the future to read, who are going through a similar thing.

I'm also hoping that my insights will be life lessons that readers can find memorable. You take any year throughout history, and any happenings in the world and in any individual's life, and you can come up with the same lessons about life, living, suffering and insight into what should make the world a better place.

The problem is that history often repeats itself, people keep making the same mistakes because they forget, and lessons seem like they never get learned! But then, we gotta keep trying and above all, hoping to make humankind better.

Anyway, "tempus fugit" [time flies] and my birthday is almost here. It's difficult to think of myself as 65. (Well, we're all getting older...but at least, better looking, right?)

John

CHAPTER 12

_____

Looking Back

I was in first year university in 1967. The era of hippies and free love. In big ways, it was a stupid and naïve era!

In 2003, I was diagnosed with chronic leukemia. Gone are the days of feeling forever young! My leukemia has remained at a low and stable level for 7 years now and maybe that is why this sense of urgency has crept up on me to finally get something written about Kenny. I never know when time's winged chariot will catch up with me.

I noticed over these few years, that I have less energy, occasionally needing to take afternoon naps. I am more achy physically and have a more fuzzy memory (not that I ever had one). I keep saying that's why I married my wife, "she's my memory." Or is that just a guy thing to forget keys and wallets and have the wife keep track of all those things? If so, then I fall right in line with other regular guys and I don't have to fret about my memory loss! My wife has trained me, and so I've made some progress in that regard about misplacing things at my advancing age of 64.

But my leukemia worries me and I've noticed my lack of energy and being more sleepy during the day. When I do something around the house, my body's batteries run down and I have to go and take a cat nap. Never used to be that way, but then I didn't have chronic leukemia before either and I wasn't 64! I identify myself more with Kenny now-a-days, because of my leukemia, an enemy within my body.

I'm more aware than ever of my own mortality. I should have been dead in 1987 at the age of 41 when my aortic valve had to be replaced with an artificial one, a Teflon St. Jude valve, size 23. Thank you, Canadian health system for the valve job which gave me a new lease on life! But it's been 24 years now and my valve has gone through a lot of mileage, clicking away every day and night, keeping me going. I don't know when another valve job will be due, so for that reason as well, I feel a sense of urgency to get something down in print about Kenny and incidentally about myself and my thoughts on living and dying and whatever the heck else crosses my mind about this crazy world.

I don't want the reproduction of the posts in Kenny's Blog and my thoughts on them to be too drab, sad and dry though. I'm hoping to present the sadness, the anger and the unfairness, as well as the empathy, the hope and even some humour in all of this, through effective and interesting writing. I will have to put on my Robert Parker uniform.

I hope my skills are up to it. I hope that there's somebody out there who might appreciate this effort, otherwise I'm singing in a vacuum with nobody out there to hear my song.

CHAPTER 13

Kenny's Blog starts with 2 posts in March 2007 talking about the tests he is scheduled for. Then there is a whole raft of posts which we've missed through spring, summer and fall. Lois' printouts pick up in winter with Marilyn's posts when Kenny could no longer do it. Her printouts end in January 2008, There are a total of 9 posts, not done by Kenny. That gap was hugely disappointing for my book. Kenny's last actual post was on December 25th, 2007, Christmas Day. He was in bad shape at 8:10 in the morning. The grammar and spelling errors are atrocious and tell of a tired mind. I got a screen capture of that post.

Here's an excerpt:

The Prodical Son returns this Christmas day!
25. December 2007 @ 08:10

HEY ALL!!! MERRY CHRISTMAS TO ALL OF YOU!!!!
I miss chatting at you all so, so, much, And it has been a heavy burden wearing on my soul that I find it hard to Blog every day like I used to. The medication I'm on still makes it VERY hard for me to focus and type – it even makes it difficult to dictate to someone else, because you tend to forget where your point was going.

Back To The Future
Wednesday, November 17, 2010

I was indecisive about what to name my book here. "If I Could Save Time?" "Time in a Bottle?" "Time's Winged Chariot?" Hmmm, "Time in a Bottle" sounds good. I will have to look for some images to create a book cover. I'm glad I inherited Kenny's software, with Dreamweaver and Fireworks, so I can design things.

When I think of Kenny's story (and mine), I think of "Time In A Bottle". There are a lot of bottle and time images in songs and poems. Jim Croce's song has always been a favourite of mine. I wanted to wrap Kenny's life and all my memories of him inside a protective enclosure, keeping Kenny dry, warm and safe, forever:

> *If I could save time in a bottle*
> *The first thing that I'd like to do*
> *Is to save every day*
> *Till eternity passes away*
> *Just to spend them with you*
>   (Jim Croce 1968)

It's, of course, a love song, the sentiment of which, in some way, was shared by the whole family who desperately did not want Kenny to die. Jim Croce was my musical idol back in the 1970s, from a generation too early for Kenny. Croce's song was already played two years on the radio by the time Kenny was born on August 5, 1970. Kenny's musical taste was flavoured with the music of a younger generation, in groups like Journey, Black Eyed Peas, Big Wreck, Toto, Econoline Crush and The Police (namely, Sting).

Sting also used the bottle imagery:

I'll send an SOS to the world
I'll send an SOS to the world
I hope that someone gets my
Message in a bottle
(Sting "Message In A Bottle" 1981)

Croce and Sting use the bottle imagery so differently but both ideas can be applied to Kenny.

Jim Croce wanted to put something inside a bottle to keep it safe forever. Sting wanted to get something out of a bottle, so that someone would read his SOS message and send him help.

In Kenny's case, that SOS was sent out to the world for 10 painful months, "Help! Cure me of cancer! I want to live!"

Kenny, felt bottled up, wanting to get out, to be read and understood by somebody, so he could be saved. His bottle, his message, never got scooped up by anybody who could actually help him. He was caught in a system. His message to the world went unanswered and he died.

Well, I've started this journey into Kenny's writing and his pain. I'll give it a rest for now, so I have a better feeling for where I am going with all these thoughts floating around inside my head.

We had "Remembrance Day" last week on November 11th 2010 and many of us remembered not only those soldiers who died in past wars (most recently in Afghanistan) but also all those loved ones who passed away in our own lives.

Lest We Forget should embrace all those who are dead and were near and dear to us. I'll plug along later to try to do justice to Kenny's memory. I'll give it a rest now. I'm run down.

I'll pull the bottle out of the ocean tomorrow, and read the SOS. I'll worry about it then.

CHAPTER 14

John's Post 4:
"The Wheel of Fortune"
Thursday, November 18, 2010

MORNING 8:30 a.m.
The big news this week has been the announcement of the royal engagement of Prince William and Kate Middleton. It should be another fairy tale wedding, this time held at Westminster Abbey, where William's mother, Princess Diana had her funeral. Her fairy tale wedding happened in 1980 with the longest train in wedding gown history. Now she is no more. The years 1980 – 2010 are a nice round 30 years. Between them, I had a traumatic break-up, made several attempts at different jobs, had two nervous breakdowns and thank goodness, married the right girl.

However, as to career and a fulfilling job? While others developed careers during those 30 years, I feel like I've been forever stuck in a crawlspace trying to dig my way out. Living should be more than just a race but it seems that is exactly what the Human Race is all about, in a competition to get ahead throughout a short lifetime.

I'd have loved it if Kenny would have taken me under wing and groomed me as a web designer but he was a genius at his craft and I don't think he had the patience to bring me along at my own pace. He also had a family to support and could do things on the computer like lightning. Well, now he's gone and the rest of us are still living, in what I call, "The Big Race." Not necessarily a Human or Humane Race.

The question on Canada AM this morning was: "Do you think that the royal marriage will last?" Answer: 82% Yes and 18% No. That was some humongous blue sapphire on Kate Middleton's finger, previously worn by Princess Di. All the jewelers in the world jumped on the bandwagon to make replicas of it and sales are already going through the roof. The same spin-off will happen with the wedding dress, royal plates and sundry knick-knacks. Well, that's the way of the world and the paparazzi will continue to have a field-day making headlines on the new royal couple who are sitting on top of the world right now. This is so reminiscent of that other beaming couple in 1980. I do hope it will go better for William and Kate.

It was also announced on Canada AM this morning that General Motors is doing quite well on the stock market. Only two years ago, it was over its head with almost $173 billion dollars in debt which made it file for bankruptcy. Hmmm, I could use a bailout right now! I just spent $1,500 in hiring Sears to clean our furnace, the ducts and installing an "electronic filter". I sure hope this will help with Marjorie's allergies; we've spent huge bucks on naturopaths and allergists (outside of the Canadian Medicare System) to help Marjorie with her wheat sensitivities and her perpetual internal nasal drainage.

Actually, the furnace guys have been banging around since 8:30 a.m., unscrewing all the vent covers and running their hoses, while I'm trying to deal with what I should say here. My brain is competing with the noise of those sucking hoses. I wonder whom Prince William and Kate Middleton will hire to clean their castle ducts, unless they move in with Grandma Elizabeth II. After all, they are a young couple just getting started! I don't know if there is a little apartment in Windsor Castle or Balmoral but then living with the royal grandmother may not be such a good idea. A castle probably has some big honkin' furnace and duct cleaning bill! A lot more than I paid for mine. But then hey, having the taxpayers' money is like having a bailout, right? Actually, my guys finished within an hour and a half but $1,500 seemed a tad high for half a morning's work.

We are victims at the hands of experts, whether we're talking about furnaces, hospitals or anything. Now, I lost my train of thought. I think I was talking about the ups and downs of life and how we are all in one huge long race until we die. Man, those guys were noisy this morning. I could hardly think to get a clear line on what I wanted to say in this entry.

We are all spinning on a *Wheel of Fortune* as time goes by. It's actually a medieval concept, the *Rota Fortunae*, referring to the capricious nature of Fate. The goddess *Fortuna* spins the wheel of life at random, changing the positions on the wheel so that some suffer great misfortune and others enjoy happy windfalls. There have been many crests and troughs throughout the past 30 years. Sometimes the ups and downs don't make sense. Death is the last trough in any person's life.

Just one week before Kenny passed away, a headline hit the news: Sir Edmund Hillary (mountain climber) – Dead. Heart attack. Died January 11, 2008. He was literally on top of the world in 1953, standing on the summit of Mt. Everest. Only one day after Kenny passed away, Suzanne Pleshette, also died from lung cancer having reached her summit in a string of Disney movies and playing Emily on *The Bob Newhart Show*. Pleshette was 71 and Hillary was 91. At least, they had a life.

They had their time and their day in the sun, and certainly more years than Kenny. Heath Ledger died 4 days after Kenny and he was only 29. He won an Academy Award posthumously for his portrayal of the Joker in *The Dark Knight*. Kenny was only 37 and he'd won the Best Web Design Award for 2007 in the Niagara Region. There weren't enough days in the sun yet for him. He should have seen more and won more awards.

There is an age when death is more acceptable than the age at which a young person dies. When someone young dies, we ask, "What might have been?" I'm not saying anything new here and certainly am not being profound about young people dying too soon. Who knows what extra musical richness Mozart might have left to the world if he would have been granted more years after the age of 35?

Kenny, besides being a superb web designer, was also a fine composer of songs and played all the accompaniments to his own music and he sang in a rich voice able to reach 4 octaves. He also stood a good chance of getting the online shopping cart contract for that popular Canadian series, *Corner Gas*, when his malady hit. He had to climb down from the ladder of success and bow out of the race. Lady Fortune is indeed capricious and can strike anybody anytime anywhere. Life's race is so short.

Kenny tried to be a positive thinker during his illness, never giving up his conviction that he would be cured, never giving up until close to the end. A few months before he passed away, in the autumn I think, he was reading *The Secret*, hoping that the positive energy from good thoughts would kick in the "law of attraction," so that the Universe would grant his wish to be healed. You could say, he rejected Fate and wanted to embrace his own Destiny. I've read somewhere: "Destiny may be seen either as a sequence of events that is inevitable and unchangeable, or that individuals choose their own destiny by choosing different paths throughout their life." Well, Kenny espoused the later idea, where he was trying to choose his own outcome and he tried, he really tried...but he was too sick and somehow he fell through the cracks in the bureaucracy of our local medical system. He became a victim on the *Wheel of Fortune*, where eventually we all will become victims, depending upon what the passage of time has done to us. Time should have cured Kenny and not have killed him.

While I write this, some people are at the top of the world and way ahead in "The Big Race." Others are making their exits from life, either with a big bang or a quiet whimper. Three years ago exactly, Kenny still had 2 months to live. There was still time to change his fate!

CHAPTER 15

Tuesday, November 18, 2010
AFTERNOON 2:00 p.m.

The sun's put a bright streak across Kenny's three paintings in the Great Room. Rainbows are dancing on the walls around the room in happy dots reflected from the Austrian crystals that I hung up in our triangular window above the sliding doors. Several of the crystals were gifts from Marjorie's dad bought at the St. Jacob's Market.

The three paintings are a modern study of a Tuscan countryside displaying green hillsides and white buildings with orange rooftops. Reminds us of the year Marjorie and I spent in France during 1988-1989 when I completed courses for a B.A. in French at the Université de Perpignan (southern France bordering the Pyrenees). Kenny gave us the paintings for Christmas 2006 but we asked Kenny to take the paintings back and tone down the brilliant yellows to make them match the muted russet and tans in our Great Room.

We didn't get the paintings back until the following year after Kenny died (when things were given back to family including keepsakes, old photo albums and of course these paintings which we stumbled upon, rummaging through old belongings in the laundry room). We noticed that Kenny had indeed toned down the brilliance of the yellows. When did he take the time to do this? We don't know but we were grateful he took the time.

I still haven't looked at Kenny's posts that Lois had printed off for us. I just don't feel the time is quite right, so I'm putting it off.

Actually I am happy that I'm writing again rearranging my thoughts in the printed word. Too bad that wasn't my "métier." Wedding photography is only gas money and I'm not sure if it will ever amount to a real career. You can't live on compliments and I'm lucky Marjorie is the bread winner for both of us.

I'm definitely not opening that plastic bag in which Kenny's posts remain hidden and dormant. Not right now! The house smells from a potent disinfectant the guys used this morning in cleaning the ducts. I'm going to flee the scene in my mint green little Accent and run chores downtown this afternoon: first the bank – pay off the credit card, take out $150 for gas and groceries, then Bulk Barn – buy quinoa and some crunchy "Garden of Eatin'" granola mix for Marjorie, go to Wintronics – buy a 25' coaxial cable and a dozen connectors, Health Food Store next – buy two boxes of cereal (Berry Sensible) for Marjorie, the Seniors' Home is on the list too – visit Uncle Walter and Harry Rittenhouse. Finally back home (hopefully the smell in the house will have dissipated by then). Ironically, cleaning the ducts was supposed to help Marjorie with her allergies. The house reeks! Maybe I'll look at Kenny's posts next week?

Okay, I'm home. *Dragnet* is on Retro TV, starring Jack Webb, badge number 714, a 1969 episode about a German shepherd, named Ginger, sniffing out marijuana. I was in third year university, writing essays, at that time, reading English Literature and history books and having a great time at the University Pub. Loved those all-night movies of Humphrey Bogart on Friday or Saturday nights at the Campus Centre. What a life! While I was indulging myself in "film noir", American kids were fighting a senseless war in Viet Nam getting killed by the Viet Cong. Whoops, I'm missing *Dragnet*! Got to stop my rambling! Tomorrow is another day and Kenny's posts can wait. So, what's the definition of procrastination?

CHAPTER 16

_____

John's Post 5:
"Destiny and Dusting"
Friday, November 19, 2010

MORNING 8:30 a.m.

One more overhead fan to dust and clean. I brought in the aluminum ladder and am dusting the house from top to bottom. Lots of cobwebs. Marjorie had a major sinus attack last night prompted by the smell in the house from the ductwork. Very strong disinfectant! Yuck. I've got the Swiffer in my left back pocket, a dust rag in my right and am lugging the shop-vac around the house sucking up cobwebs here and there. I consider this my bi-yearly job (I just hate dusting). I don't consider this my destiny but if I do go to hell, I know exactly what my punishment will be. I swore to myself we won't ever get the ducts cleaned again.

Marjorie came home at about 8:30 p.m. yesterday, Thursday night, after a fatiguing stint of Parent/ Teacher interviews. She's great at mimicking unreasonable parents who aren't satisfied with a decent kid getting a B or B+: "I know my child should be getting an A, so you give him that!" Lots of finger pointing. The kid is doing nicely in Marjorie's class and is a really decent kid but if he would get 99%, mom would want to know from the kid, "Where's the other 1%?"

Marjorie told the parent that kids still need to be kids and that is why she also does not give her grade 6s and 7s homework over the weekends because that's kid time and family time. The dad was upset because there wasn't any homework over the weekends.

> "You can't please everyone, so you've gotta please yourself!"
> (Rick Nelson, Garden Party, 1972)

Thank goodness, Marjorie has the grit to stand up to parents. There's so much pressure on teachers. A lot of them give in thinking that the confrontation is just not worth it. They knuckle under, marks are puffed up and standards go down the tube.

Marjorie was very fatigued when she came home and then faced that sinus attack in the middle of the night from the lingering smell of the ductwork. Her usual wake-up time is 5:45 a.m. which comes way too early, especially when you don't sleep well. It was very difficult this morning. I got up with her and chopped up 23 almonds for her breakfast, got the oatmeal going and packed her lunch, while she walked on the treadmill and then washed her hair.

I'm picking Marjorie up at the school later this afternoon, at 4:00 p.m. I usually sit and read a book until 5:00 p.m., while she lesson plans for the next teaching day, which, in this case, is Monday. No other teacher is in the building at 5:00 p.m.

On Fridays, we have a special arrangement with Maryjane, the Kindergarten teacher, who meets us in the driveway of the Experimental Farm and then takes Marjorie to school the rest of the way. That's Marjorie's social time with Maryjane, who is also a playwright in her spare time. While they drive off to school together, I go home to work on my web sites, my photography or if a guilty conscience hits me, do housework and run chores.

Well, the dusting still has to be done (it's a dirty job, but somebody's got to do it).   One more overhead fan to do! Achoo!!!

AFTERNOON

I watched *Peter Gunn* (1960) over lunch hour, munching a sandwich (leftover meats from supper at last night's Parent/ Teacher interviews). At least I don't have to listen to sucking air hoses in the ducts while I clear my thoughts for this afternoon's writing. I've got all the doors open and the overhead fans going to air out the rooms.

Children's voices are filtering in from next door through our open sliding doors in the Great Room. Denise runs a Day Care and has a playground set up in her backyard. She does a terrific job by giving the kids a regular play schedule.   The little voices are actually calming me down as I think about what to write about us, Kenny and me. I think about Kenny's kids. They were 6 and 2 when Kenny died. Darriane is a little starlette and Braeden is a little ham. We're seeing them again this coming Sunday, so Darriane can light a remembrance candle for daddy.

It's funny seeing *Peter Gunn*, filmed in black and white, but broken up by colour commercials. I guess stringing those coaxial cables along the joists in the crawlspace was worth it after all, one line for the front TV and one line for the back TV in the Great Room. I felt like a soldier in the crawlspace, scraping along on my tummy in enemy territory. Had to keep my butt down, otherwise lift it a little and I'd bang myself on a furnace duct or a joist. Ouch!   My work down there is not good for my sciatic nerve or the arthritis in my shoulders but hey, we can watch HD TV without paying the cable company! Surely that satisfaction is worth something!

I must admit the commercials they put on during *Peter Gunn* are pretty tacky and tell a lot about the broken society, especially in the United States. Obama hasn't solved anything in my opinion.

There's Humana with all-in-one Medicare (if you have the money); AARP insurance to supplement your regular medicare (which is extra money).

If all these options with Plans A, B and C, get confusing, fear not! The middle man has popped up to fill this need like a bad weed.

Health market services will find you the perfect medical plan which meets your need, and your budget, and which saves you money! Your insurance marketplace will do it all for you, so you don't have to struggle through the paperwork, and all the confusing options and legalese in Medicare and Medicaid plans.

What do you think is behind all these "services" that take care of you to simplify things for you when you shop around for the perfect plan? It's money! Apparently, the consultation fee is free, but that can lead to signing up for unwanted plans which lead to other fees you did not count on, so there are complaints with the Better Business Bureau against unscrupulous agents.

I get suspicious about "free" services, because those free favours hide behind American greed and the motivation of profit and money, lawyers and lawsuits. They don't take care of you. They take care of themselves! What a convoluted system!

I'm sure when Kenny did research on his computer when he had his cancer, all these things in the medical profession and its services unravelled for him like a horrifying reality, aspects of which ignited his anger so he would rage at what seemed like a helpless situation – which it was!

There are commercials about DePuy Hip Replacements, which have left people crippled so that the Johnson Law Group is also advertising in commercials on TV for litigants to get them the compensation they deserve, and finally there's a free book (no obligation) if you suffer from "Mesothelioma" (more lawyers looking for clients). I Googled mesothelioma – it's cancer from asbestos and the source says, "Compensation via asbestos funds or lawsuits is an important issue in mesothelioma (see asbestos and the law)."

Oasis Legal Finance is another example, in my opinion, of the United States being in deep trouble where people are duped into more debt. They promise money up front, so you don't have to be kept waiting in the court system to tide you over until you actually win the compensation "you deserve." They are banking on the possibility of a buck from the courts and that's just plain stupid.

Drug companies have grown smart over the past few years and now, there are all sorts of disclaimers about side effects. How can the Food and Drug Administration (FDA) pass all these drugs which can make things worse than what they are supposed to cure!

What a society!

Law firms, pharmacies, insurance companies and medical providers, all looking to give clients things they deserve! Those services are like a house of cards ready to fall apart at the slightest sneeze. What if the government bailouts don't succeed and an actual Great Depression crumbled the economy in the States? The public consumer is really stupid in America.

And where their IQ is low, their obesity is high, Just don't get me started!

eDiets.com delivers 7 full days of meals plus snacks and claims that people can lose 40 pounds, 60 pounds, 94 pounds. Heck, a responsible person should be able to buy their own healthy foods and save themselves wheelbarrow full of money. I could see people buying extra snacks in between the portions that the diet companies deliver! How many failures do they have? But maybe it's like wedding photographers. They don't show the bad pictures to get more clients, they only show the good ones. [Of course, mine are mostly good!]

Kirstie Alley has disappeared from the Jenny Craig commercials only to be replaced by a perky Valerie Bertinelli who lost 47 pounds. I wonder if the two are still friends? Pills, diets, exercise gimmicks and hypnosis!

The social problem is pervasive from teens to adults and it's a booming business in the States! Look out Canada; we're just next door! A recent email forwarded to me said that Americans had terrible food habits and also didn't understand how their bodies worked:

> America is an obese nation. The CDC states that one out of every three Americans is considered obese (i.e. weighs 30% more than his normal weight). Ever wonder why? Well, part of it is that we are a nation of gluttons and sluggards. Self-control is considered passé. However, part of the reason for America's obesity is the fact that our diet typically is 90% cooked foods. Hog farmers learned a long time ago that hogs get fat twice as fast if they are fed cooked food. Cooking destroys what? You got it...**enzymes**.

But hey, with two parents working (or on welfare), people are too busy to cook properly and the easy out is McDonald's and Tim Horton's Doughnuts.

When I worked as a reporter, years ago in Chilliwack B.C., a new McDonald's outlet came to town and the manager told me that it was a real boon to the community because previously kids would pester their parents into driving 60 miles into Vancouver just to get a Big Mac. He made a booming business in that little town drawing in the kids, parents and seniors from all over the Fraser Valley.

I suppose fast foods have their place but they've become a mainstay as "staple foods" in our rushed society.

And it's not just what Americans digest physically that's bad; it's also their intake of TV commercials and drugs.

Big Business and Big Government are making something out of nothing for American consumers. Paper money is printed off in the billions and injected into companies that should have gone broke because of mismanagement, like General Motors. Who can forget the CEOs from GM flying into Washington in their private jets to ask for bailout loans? To fly in on private jets took some gall, or was just plain ignorant! Now that they are bailed out, have they changed their lifestyles?

Tacky commercials are small signs of the bigger problem which is, that the economy in the States is sick and people are stupid enough to buy anything.

But for me, suffering through all the tripe in these commercials is still worth it, to watch my current favourite crime show, *Peter Gunn,* in black and white. I don't think Kenny would have liked it though; he was more into the techno stuff in modern movies. He would have loved *Avatar* (which I haven't seen yet).

CHAPTER 17

Next week for sure

I'm still trying to prime myself into actually looking at those printouts in the plastic bag. This week is out. Next week for sure!

Almost time to pick Marjorie up at the school; then the weekend is here. I'm seeing Dr. M. (our family physician) on Saturday morning to get my INR (blood thinness) checked and then Sunday, Darriane will light her candle for her daddy. In the evening, I am doing media for the church since the Niagara Men's Chorus is singing there. When I was handling media last week after the church service, Darriane came up to me when I was shutting down the computer and said, "My daddy would have been good at that." "Yes," I said, "he would have been terrific. He was a computer geek."

Saturday November 20, 2010
Since yesterday, I already put in two calls to Sears Indoor Air Cleaning Services to let them know that Marjorie had a terrible sinus attack from their services.

They finally called back on this Saturday morning, a fellow with a heavy East Indian accent whom I could hardly understand, telling me they've never had any complaints like that before, that the disinfectant they blow through ducts is what they use in hospitals.

I told him that Sears should give a caution, in a house where somebody has extreme allergies, that the house will smell for a couple of days, that the person with allergies should sleep overnight at a relative's and that the house should be aired out for a couple of hours with the windows and doors open.

I thanked him for the call, he thanked me and I'm sure after he hung up, he promptly forgot all about the complaint. My concern will never be made policy with the cleaning crews because they've never had any complaints before. So much for the chain of checks and balances in any "bureaucrapic" system.

I mentioned the ups and downs of life a while ago. I just heard that Pat Burns died yesterday, Friday November 19, of cancer. He was the former NHL coach who led the New Jersey Devils to the 2003 Stanley Cup title. Doctors discovered he had colon cancer in 2004, which spread to his liver and then in 2009 spread to his lungs. He was 58. Fate should be called the Wheel of Misfortune, not the Wheel of Fortune. But at least Pat Burns had 21 years more time than Kenny.

Addendum Tues. Nov. 30, 2010 - News flash:

"Thieves broke into the car of Pat Burns' widow Tuesday, just hours after the NHL coaching legend was laid to rest, stealing family photos, personal effects and hockey memorabilia.

Even the bed sheets from the palliative-care unit where Burns spent his final days were taken from Line Burns, the wife's car in the early morning theft, police said Tuesday."

Pat Burns' family pleads for the return of stolen mementos
    (CTV.ca News Staff)

Robin Burns, Pat's cousin had delivered the eulogy earlier that day. He called the act deplorable and said that the thieves had no conscience.

Unfortunately, a conscience gets left behind when it comes to the haves and have-nots in this world or where greed sees the chance to make a quick buck. Of course, the thieves had no conscience; that is why they are thieves. Doing something like this is comparable to the porno people dumping hundreds of porno links into the comment boxes in Kenny's Blog and then causing us to spend hours searching for and deleting all those inappropriate links.

There are people that are just plain bad people in the world. And yet, these people once were children themselves and had parents who should have taught them right from wrong.

Who knows how people get off on the wrong track? It doesn't make life any easier for others. I can see theft being necessary where hunger is concerned, as in the case of Jean Valjean stealing bread in *Les Miserables* but stealing family memorabilia from Pat Burns' car? That's just plain low!

My migraine headache has finally dissipated. Marjorie is watching her cooking shows now on WNED (thanks to me for running cables in the crawlspace).

I watched my favourite morning cartoon, *My Goldfish Is Evil*, (which can only be a Canadian production but somehow I'm hooked on it).

Dr. M. also took my blood sample and told me his son was in 3rd year computer programming at the University of Waterloo and has been promised a job already. Ah, to be young, talented and healthy and to be at the start of your life!

We're going grocery shopping after lunch and then I'm making Marjorie's mom's delicious bean casserole and the gluten free chocolate fudge cake for the pot-luck tomorrow after church. We pick Kenny's kids up at 9:00 a.m. Braeden is 5 now and Darriane is 9 years old.

CHAPTER 18

John's Post 6:
"Goldfish Crackers and Peace"
Sunday November 21, 2010

Braeden had the flu and so only Darriane came with us to church to light the candle for her daddy.

Braeden was drenched from fever last night and mom was hoping that it was only the flu and not extra infection from the recent ruptured appendix and the operation that cleared out the poison. We don't need another crisis in the family, certainly not so soon.

There were 10 other people who also lit candles for loved ones. Darriane did a great job in front of the church when her name was called and I quickly snapped a picture or two, so mommy and Braeden could see. Marjorie had prepared an activity bag for her to keep her busy during the sermon. The bag had a container of goldfish crackers (cheese flavoured) and some paper and crayons for drawing. Darriane drew a bunch of peace symbols (her favourite thing now). How fads go in full circles! Does anybody remember the '60s? Now Darriane collects all kinds of clothing and knick-knacks emblazoned with the peace symbol.

After lunch, we drove over to Marjorie's sister's place to visit Bria, the little dog who loves to have her tummy scratched. And then we drove Darriane back home.

On the way, Darriane asked all sorts of questions about her daddy and about Marjorie's mom. Marjorie is very wise about answering a little girl's questions dealing with sensitive issues. Her 24 year-old cousin, Andrew, is getting baptized next Sunday at St. Ann's Community Church. Darriane wanted to know what baptism was. She asked how old her daddy was when he was baptized. She wanted to be baptized because her daddy was baptized. We told her that this was not a good enough reason, that she needed to get older and make that decision on her own and not just because her daddy did it. She asked about her daddy's mom and how old she was when she died...and why she died. "That was my mom too," Marjorie explained. "Your daddy was 10 years old." Marjorie told her that her grandmother, Laura, died because of a heart problem.

Actually, during an operation for a faulty mitral valve, the operator made a mistake on the heart-lung machine, which pumped air into her system which killed her. The hospital tried to cover the mistake up but everything came to light with probing questions from the family physician. We didn't go into all that with Darriane, simply explaining that her grandmother died because of a sick heart. It amazed me how inquisitive and persistent a little girl, 9 years of age, can be in digging up the past. The situation was almost uncomfortable and Marjorie was honest but very tactful.

I don't know if I can finish this book! But who will? It's too painful for dad.

Everybody else in the family has moved on and is too busy with their own lives, mostly with jobs. Marilyn, is running the office at a dental clinic, Marjorie, is a grade 6/ 7 teacher, and Sue, has been promoted from case worker to assistant manager for the Red

Cross. Nobody has the time or even the desire to unravel Kenny's story and I don't know if I can do justice to it. How many layers do I expose in this story, not only about Kenny but also about myself?

I wish I had a better memory for recalling the context and the dialogue between Marjorie, myself and Darriane during that drive back to her mom's house. But that's the way it is. Ya got whatcha got, and someday you're gonna lose it all anyway!

I really don't know if I can do this? And I haven't even touched those printouts yet. The printouts are lying there in a plastic bag behind my old 1966 yearbooks.

I made a screen capture of only two pages of Kenny's Blog myself, just the ones entitled, "**I Rage**" and "**Prodical Son Returns**."
I've got snippets of the Blog. Then, there's the first two pages I salvaged of Ken's personal web site, so that we have something of "kenjanzen.com" (which no longer exists).

I've already printed those pages out and threw them in with the bundle that Lois gave us from the Blog. It's just difficult to sort through this stack of pages and get started retyping everything into the computer. That will be an arduous, tedious and also painful task!

It's raining outside now; it's snowing in Alberta; and I'm still not courageous enough to face the past. November 2010 is almost over, now it's 3 years later!

I close my eyes
only for a moment
and the moments gone
all my dreams
pass before my eyes a curiosity

dust in the wind
all we are is dust in the wind
(Kansas, 1977)

CHAPTER 19

John's Post 7 [retyped]:
"Kenny Introduces Kenny"

a bit about me

Well, by now you probably guessed my name – that's right, Ken Janzen. And you might be wondering about the whole citrus fruit on my website thing. Well, I figured this site is a little...wait for it..."Slice" of my life that I'm making available to all of you.

Why would I wanna splatter my personal life all over the net you ask...because I feel that I have been truly blessed and want to share a little bit about me and my wonderful family and friends with those of you that are interested.

Quick facts

Born Aug. 5, 1970

So that makes me 35 years of age

Married: Yep – to my beautiful wife, Sue.

Children: Darriane – she's soooo cute. Braeden – our newest arrival.

Likes: Pulling all nighters in front of the 'puter and of course. Coffee – lots of coffee.

Dislikes: When there's no coffee – WHAT! No Coffee!! Mornings in general – yuk!!

Hobbies: Woodworking, Writing and performing music, golf and lots of other stuff I wish I had more time to do.

Favourite Colour: Purple (and no – I don't know why...)

Favourite Clothing: Brüzer – They make killer duds.
Favourite Bands: *Big Wreck, the Black Eyed Peas, Sting, Toto, Econoline Crush, Journey* and many more.
Favourite Movies: *The Fifth Element, Men in Black, Schrek, Independence Day, Hunt for Red October*.
Favourite Author: Tom Clancy (I think I have all his books – really...
How I spend my spare time: Just hangin' out with my family & friends, playing Xbox & GameCube or just watching a movie.

A long time ago...
Hmmmm. A brief history...where do I start...
I was born in St. Catharines, Ontario and was adopted at 10 weeks by Wally and Laura Janzen. Grew up in Attercliffe (basically in the middle of nowhere, Ontario) and went to public school at Caistor Centre Public School. At this point I guess I was your typical kid, albeit one with good grades (both parents being teachers – I had no choice).

At the age of 14, the family moved to Beamsville while our new house in Fonthill was being built. I went to Beamsville High School until 1987. When we finally moved into the new house, I transferred to E.L. Crossley Secondary School in Fonthill and graduated in 1989, with honours no less...what a geek...
While in high school, I played in a band that won a few contests and had a few gigs. Ahhh...the first taste of the spotlight. I guess that's why I went and got certified as a recording engineer – loved the whole music thing and wanted to learn more. After college, I went on the road for a while and played keys and sang in a band that played all over Ontario – life on the road – riiiight!!
Met my beautiful wife Sue in 1992 how else? I was playing in a band...but now that I had a serious relationship and an upcoming wedding – I had to grow up a bit...so I got a regular day job – for a while....

In 1997 I got my grubby paws on one of those new fangled computer thingys and started playing around – and the rest is history. I guess I always had a knack for art and music, but the computer has allowed me to express myself in ways I never thought possible even 5 years ago.

What's up now

Nowadays I spend most of my time in front of this infernal computer, doing what I love to do – create websites. In 2000 I co-founded a web design company – *Effective Design Solutions* – with my best bud Frank Pizzacalla and after 2 years of successful operations, we decided to sell the business to pursue our individual dreams and goals. From 2002 – 2004, I was the Creative Director at *Target Internet Development* here in St. Catharines, and now – who knows what's gonna happen!
On top of all this, I recently became a dad again! My daughter Darriane Laura Janzen was born on Sept. 7, 2001, and now our son, Braeden Christopher Janzen was born on August 5, 2005 (yup – the little bugger was born on my birthday!).

What does the future hold? Who knows. Check back here for periodic updates and thanks for visiting my site!!
  Salvaged Excerpt: kenjanzen.com (2002) .... now defunct

CHAPTER 20

John's Doubts About a Blog

"Oh Yeah, The Boy Can Play"
(Dire Straits 1985)
Monday, November 22, 2010

It's the Feast Day of Saint Cecelia, patron saint of musicians. So it's especially apt to remember Kenny on this day. He had a 4 octave range, composed music and sang his own songs, played the keyboard and recorded his own mix.

His dad's favourite story is about a family get-together when Kenny was a toddler, where he'd bop in rhythm to a jazz record Uncle Gerry Ediger put on at Grandpa's house. When the music stopped, he'd stop; when the music was started, Kenny would sway to the beat, again oblivious to surroundings.

Kenny loved the piano and hated lessons. He'd con his teacher into playing the piece so nicely for him once and then he wouldn't practice all week but when he went to the next lesson, he'd play the piece perfectly. "Just play it for me once," he'd say to his teacher.

Dad belonged to the St. Ann's Choir and brought Kenny along as a 13 year old to the practices. Pete Martens the choir director permitted Kenny to sit with the tenors. When dad asked Pete if Kenny helped or hindered, Pete remarked, "Kenny IS the tenor section!"

Kenny could also wiggle the lobs of his ears and his nostrils, so that the family was always entertained with his weird peripheral talents. He had a sense of humour and did a great job imitating elderly men. I made him an "honorary geezer" one year. We felt that he mistreated his vocal chords by smoking cigarettes like a smoke stack, but there was nothing we could say or do about that.

We were all so proud of him when he made his first (and only CD), *My Sentiments Exactly* in 2007. Kenny had copies of his songs and singing on his computer from earlier efforts and he (and we)

were lucky he had done that. The first thing that went, when his lung cancer surfaced, was his voice. He could only whisper in a broken raspy way. His larynx was "frozen" in a certain spot. His singing was gone and for a singer with such talent, that was mental anguish to accept. Yet Kenny worked on what he had recorded earlier and persisted in producing his first CD. He wrote on the cover: "Most of the songs on this CD were written and recorded by me because of specific emotional events that I have experienced in my life over the past 15 years. I always seem to turn to my music to express my feelings and hence, my original songs were written for joyful times like births, weddings and anniversaries and also for sad events like funerals. Thank you for taking the time to share my sentiments – my sentiments exactly!" Adam Martin and Frank Pizzacalla contributed their guitar skills to Kenny's CD.

*****

So In Love:
So in Love, when I see you standing beside me
So in Love, won't you come & share your life with me

My Little Baby Girl:
When I first held you in my arms
I swore I'd shelter you from harm
I'd protect my baby girl

Dear Daddy:
When I was a child I found my place
Sheltered by your warm embrace
When I was a child I saw your smiling face
Look down on me bouncing on your knee...
I am a better man because of you
I will proudly stand beside you...

Oma's Song:
There was never a harsh word
Only kindness in your eyes...
I look over and expect to see you
But the good Lord took you home...

Epilogue (Opa's Song):
Remember the laughter – through the tears
A soul takes flight on wings of angels
But memories never disappear

Through the years you'll always be here in my heart
You'll be singing – with the angels – tonight...

$$*****$$

There are little photos, little jewels of memories, interspersed among the lyrics of the songs on the CD jacket: Dad (Wally) & Ken circa 1971. Mom (Laura) & Ken circa 1974. Oma & Opa Boldt circa 1986. Ken & Frank '05. Adam & Ken '05. The Janzen Family: Ken & Sue '95 wedding photo. Ken & Sue '06. Darriane '06 aka "Sweets". Braeden '07 aka "Pucker-Boy."

Ken wrote this dedication on our copy of his CD: "Love ya Guys! Kenny!" Braeden asks to play his dad's CD occasionally when the kids visit Aunt Marjorie and Uncle John, but Darriane, I think, is still hurting about why her daddy had to die and she doesn't ask for the CD to be played. She has said to my wife: "When God wasn't in our house, daddy was healthy. When God came into our house, daddy got sick." That's the cause and effect she sees in her child's mind and in fact, an adult might see it that way too, and utterly hate God for taking Kenny away.

I like to think that Kenny still lives on in an alternate universe, that he didn't get sick and that the dream he might have had in his coma during his last few days was of himself living out a full life with Sue and the kids. Maybe he's waiting there in that alternate universe somewhere sometime for us.

A favourite song of his was sung at his funeral by one of his best buddies, Adam.

>   *Wherever you go*
>   *Whatever you do*
>   *I will be right here waiting for you*

My Brother-in-Law
Got Sick

Whatever it takes
Or how my heart breaks
I will be right here waiting for you
(Bryan Adams 2006)

CHAPTER 21

Disappointment and Rage

When I took a quick peek at the pages we "salvaged" from Kenny's Blog, I was disappointed. It was truly a paltry handful of pages, compared to the nuggets I expected that would be saved for a book. There's so little of his written thoughts there in Lois' printouts, that I kept asking if I should just abandon this wintery project. I had to go in a different direction now, so that I could squeeze some kind of book out of all the bits and pieces I had.

The printouts go from October 12th 2007 (3 short months before Kenny died) to January 23rd summing up the aftermath of the funeral, by his youngest sister, Marilyn, and by his wife, Sue. Kenny's last post was December 25th 2007, Christmas Day, which I thankfully had also made a screen capture of, so I actually got two of the Blog's important pages for sure, April 27, 2007, **And I Rage** and December 25, 2007, **The Return of the Prodical Son**.

But the majority of the spring, summer and autumn posts were lost, disappeared in the virtual reality that is known as the internet. We have nothing from a big stretch of that time in *Ken Janzen's Health and Wellness Blog*.

Most of what he himself wrote and thought stretched from March 2007 to October 2007 and the family sadly had nothing of that saved!

It's too bad, because most of what he wrote through that time as I recall was punchy and clear, expressed in Kenny's inimitable style and was shaping up to what could have been a remarkable book about how he felt plagued by cancer, about the slow waiting times in the system, and his questions about God. I will have to see what I snagged in those Snippets I copied and pasted into a file from those months because I'm not even sure what I collected anymore.

I'm not blaming Lois; she saved what was important to her at the time, which was basically some posts written during the last few months of the Blog, where Kenny went downhill and Marilyn had to take over posting.

At the moment, I simply don't know how to reconstruct the missing pieces and to use the patchwork of these later printouts to create a salvageable book about Kenny's journey.

Maybe there are some hidden pearls of wisdom in the crumbs that are left. Who knows what else resides in those snippets that I hastily copied. You never know, these little seeds may yet germinate into a lovely flower.

I nearly missed *Peter Gunn* at lunch time. I had to put dad's cooking pot outside the door. Judy will pick it up so dad can make his famous borscht for Andrew's baptism. I'm making my chili. Had my first unsolicited comment in my Blog. That worries me. It was from some internet address (url) with the words "colon cleansing" in it. I've let nobody know about my Blog, yet they found me and they can't even spell! "Thanks for an idea, you sparked at thought from a angle I hadn't given thought to yet. Now lets see if I can do something with it." I changed the address of my Blog so that "The webpage cannot be found." Grrrr! How do people find my stuff when I wanted to keep my writing about Kenny private until I was ready?

I've got another migraine headache today. I've suffered from them since I was 16. I remember excusing myself from history class to go to the washroom to vomit. I would get that distracting aura, where things flashed and twinkled before my eyes, where I saw only half of a person's faces, and then half an hour later, the pain would hit, escalate until the 3rd hour and then slowly recede until the 8th hour.

I would have to go home, lie down in a dark room and cover my head with a pillow. This often happened around exam time when I was a teenager. When I was 19, my family physician gave me "ergodryl" which made me loopy enough through the day to take the edge off the pain. His comforting comment was that intelligent people usually get migraines and that they often disappeared when a person hit his mid 50s. Of course being 19 at the time, and often in pain, I was not comforted by that observation. Now that I'm 64, I still get the occasional aura and the pain has become less excruciating, nor is the headache as long lasting as in my youth. I now call my migraines weather headaches which I feel are related to the barometric pressure.

Unfortunately, sometimes the condition arises even when the weather is changing to a sunny day, not necessarily a rainy day. But as Frank Sinatra says, "That's life!"

I was really ticked off about that first comment being lodged on my Blog unsolicited. I trashed it. Grrrr! Somehow it reminded me of all those porno links that were dumped into the comment boxes in Kenny's Blog during 2007. How crass was that! I've got to lie down a bit to rest my head.

Smoke Gets in your Eyes

Kenny was a heavy smoker. He kept himself pumped up for his work by chain smoking and drinking coffee, cup after cup, after cup. When he visited us to fix something on our computer, he always cradled a Timmy's cup in his hand.

I snickered at the commercial during the *Peter Gunn* episode: EZsmoker! It promoted a fake cigarette without the ash, flame or tar of a real cigarette. There's a sensor with a heat element that releases an odourless vapour that's supposed to be harmless. The tip of the cigarette even glows, so it gives a realistic experience. What a joke! It reminded me of the candy cigarettes you used to get for a nickel at the corner store when I was a kid.

EZsmoker could be sold for $150 but all you have to pay is shipping and processing. Of course, who knows how much that is? All you have to do is phone this easy 1-800 number. Kenny had a couple of ashtrays on his veranda right next to the barbecue, laden with a big litter of cigarette butts. His house just reeked of cigarettes and Marjorie had problems there with her allergies. But hey, if we wanted to visit, it was his house! Kenny stopped smoking in the spring of 2007 two weeks before he was diagnosed with lung cancer. That was a most cruel and unjust irony.

Just about everybody smokes in the old *Peter Gunn* episodes, including Peter Gunn. I guess it was fashionable in those days, even for the ladies. It figures since Peter Gunn's girlfriend, Edie, owned a nightclub and was the featured soloist each night while patrons ate, drank and had a leisurely smoke. How many countless lives did cigarettes cost in those black and white movie days, because it was the cool thing to do?

I've discovered a treasure trove which will help me flesh out a book on Kenny's lymphoma, my own leukemia and Anwar Knight's Blog about what he is going through with his cancer. Anwar is the weather guy on CTV Toronto. His TV station created a Blog for him through their web site after he found out in May 2010 that he had Hodgkin's Lymphoma. It's a well written Blog which expresses so many of the same feelings that Kenny had in his Blog, three years earlier.

So I've gotten several different perspectives from which I can look at Kenny's journey: his, mine and Anwar's. I intend to travel back and forth in time and comb over Kenny's last 10 months several times over, like looking for different shells on the beach, the more times you wander over the same area, the more precious shells you find. I hope that any repetitions might just yield a shell with a slightly different colour and shape. There's so many hidden and valuable memories that wash up in a person's life when you look back time and time again.

CHAPTER 22

———————————

I'm liking the Blog idea for myself less and less. Though the comments going into Kenny's Blog were encouraging, they were in terms of literary substance, not really useful. I might also run the risk of getting a bunch of unsolicited links thrown into the comment boxes, which is what happened to Kenny's Blog where some hacker threw in hundreds of porno links.

Therefore, I'm thinking more of a book now, using the posts in Kenny's Blog and my diary notations as the core for a book. There should be enough to say about cancer, living and dying with it that people could identify and find interesting. It's most fitting to start with Kenny's anger about his diagnosis. He was really fuming about the cards that fate had dealt him. "Why me?"

*****

Kenny's Post

This is what he wrote in April 2007, a month after he started his Blog and a month after he was diagnosed with lung cancer:

And I Rage!
27. April 2007 @ 14:21
Today is another one of those very bad days.

I have been given my official prognosis by my oncologist and with much sorrow I will share it with you now. If I had no conventional treatment (chemo) they give me 6 months to live. With chemo that number jumps to a *whopping* 12-18 months.

So I sit here typing and I RAGE!!! In between the bouts of tears I RAGE! I clench my fists till I can clench no more – I shake those fists at the heavens and shout to the Lord; "Why?!", "Why Me?!" "Why should my beautiful 5 year old daughter and wonderful 20 month old son have to grow up without me as their father?!", "Why should I have to be the one to have to leave my beautiful wife, my soul-mate and best friend?", "Why am I the one who has to leave all my friends behind?", "Was I not good enough? Living enough, caring enough?"....and I RAGE!!! I rage until I cannot handle the wracking pain of my sobs anymore.

And I suppose this is a natural reaction, as I am only human and trying to seek answers where there are no obvious answers to be had. All I can do now is trust that God does have a plan for me and my family.

Please forgive me! I have not given up. Not by a long shot! It's just that coming to terms with your own mortality in light of a really poor prognosis can make even the most positive (and humorous) of us crack under pressure.

Please know that I love you all and I wonder if I could beg something of you all just one more time?...Please say a little prayer for hope, re-assurance, calm, and peace. We could all use a little of each of those right now.

For those of you who are local – please feel free to drop by anytime over this coming weekend and beyond. We would love to see you!

*****

Introspection by John

November 23, 2010
MORNING
The subtitle of Ken's Wellness Blog was *"The Medical Mystery that is Me."* There were 25 comments in this post where he raged. Jen Rogalsky, his cousin in Winnipeg, was the first to comment: "Oh, my dear Kenny. I'll change the words a bit to a song that keeps running through my head: 'I will weep when you are weeping. When you rage I'll rage with you.' I love you, Jen."

There were no other comments salvaged with this printout. Ken was understandably cynical about his prognosis where he seemed to sneer at the number of months he was given to live, "jumping" up to a "whopping" 12-18 months if he had chemo.

I could see him raging, walking in circles in an agitated state in his office downstairs, computer screen lit up in front of him on the desk, where he did his creative work on web sites, the work he had such a great talent and passion for, the work that was now being shut down on him by something beyond his control, by something he did not ask for. In the months to come, Kenny had to tell his clients that he could no longer service their web sites. He made CD copies of sites and gave them to his clients telling them to find another hosting company and web designer. He was unraveling all that he had built over the years, his future and his source of income. But for now, he was just plain pissed off and like a caged animal in the basement, he raged to get out of the trap he was in.

He also cried until he could cry no more. And then the cycle would repeat. He called upon God. All of this was a natural reaction and looking for answers, he could find none. He mentions his sense of humour which he had in abundance but even that disappears when you crack under more pressure than you can handle because you were told you only have months to live.

One of the snippets I saved from the Blog is applicable here. I decided to copy the title, the date and time from the original post and also to copy the number of comments it elicited, giving it a sense of reality from the Blog. Pretend you zoomed into Kenny's Blog from somewhere up above like Google Earth and then zoomed back into this book to analyze the entry.

Life Experiences
5. August 2007 @ 13:30

In the Bible it talks about how our experiences now prepare us for our future and how God does not give us more challenges than we can handle at any one time

Maybe I'm suffering because God wanted me to slow down and start my non-profit foundation. Or, maybe my suffering is entirely moot and I will gain nothing.

Till Tomorrow All!
The Medical Mystery that is Me :) | Comments (26)

Like most Christians, Kenny misinterpreted the passage in The New Testament, 1 Corinthians 10:13, where people think God will not give them more suffering than they can bear but that is not what it means!

What the Bible says is: "God is faithful. He will not allow the <u>temptation</u> to be more than you can stand. When you are tempted, he will show you a way out so that you can endure." So it talks about temptation and not suffering! I think God actually allows the world to give you more suffering than you can bear, and that's the world, not God's wish.

I believe that prayer helps to soothe the anguished soul. Kenny reached out to other people for emotional support, even with little prayers, because he felt so alone, desperate and angry. He was looking for re-assurance, calm and peace in that storm raging inside of himself.

He wanted people to visit him, the presence of other human beings to keep him company and distract him from raging storm inside of him. Friends and relatives in fact came in and out of the Janzen home whenever they could from April on when he raged, which soothed his angry soul during those dark days and nights in the spring of 2007 when fruit trees blossomed outside in all their colourful splendour in the Niagara Region.

CHAPTER 23

Dark Night of the Soul

In those months, through spring, summer, autumn and winter, Kenny must have experienced many a "dark night of the soul."

(The term "dark night of the soul" is used in Christianity for a spiritual crisis in a journey towards union with God, like that described by Saint John of the Cross, a 16th century Spanish poet.) Jesus must have felt the same in the Garden of Gethsemane before his crucifixion, to the point of sweating droplets of blood from the stress of knowing how he was going to die. (This condition is medically possible, called "*hematohidrosis*.")

Maybe we all face a dark night of the soul at some point (provided Alzheimer's hasn't hit us yet). During those nights and days, after Kenny heard the pronouncement "cancer", he must have felt so isolated downstairs on that couch, trapped in his own body, feeling like an island with no rescue boat in sight.

Had he lived in Elizabethan England, Kenny might have become friends with John Donne or even become another John Donne, himself, because he had a poet's talent. Instead of being a computer geek, he might have been a minstrel. Instead of a Blog, Kenny might have penned this poem: "No man is an island, entire of itself every man is a piece of the continent...never send to know for whom the bell tolls it tolls for thee."

John Donne (d. 1631) wrote these lines looking out of his window, recuperating from tuberculosis. Some say that Donne finally died of stomach cancer.

As Donne got older, he wrote works that challenged death. He wrote about the fear that it inspired in many men but he believed strongly that those who die are sent to heaven to live eternally. "Death, be not proud, though some have called thee Mighty and dreadful, for thou art not so." – (Holy Sonnet X)

Kenny had the feistiness to challenge death so many times during those months of his illness. Near the end, he gave himself more to a hope in God because fighting his illness on his own just got beyond him.

I'm split on the idea of "no man is an island." We are each of us alone at the end of our life to face death. It was Kenny who had to face his own end, even though family was gathered around his death bed. We each felt like an island in our own sorrow and grief and yet we were not alone because we also shared it. What a paradox!

It was in this April 27 post, **And I Rage**, in which I made a lengthy comment about Dylan Thomas, the Welsh poet, having enough pluck to rage against death. I can't remember exactly what I said; my writing is lost.

I think I told Kenny that he was quite right to rage and that he showed courage in doing so and that this was a good sign for him to be so outraged. And I left it at that.

After I witnessed Kenny's death by his bedside on January 18, 2008, I could have added more insights about Dylan Thomas and John Donne, were it possible to go back in time. But that was not the thing to do earlier in the Blog because comments were meant to be tactful there and encouraging at the time.

*****

Thomas, like Donne (and Kenny no less), was very angry about the human condition, which means suffering and mortality.

> *Do not go gentle into that good night*
> *Old age should burn and rave at close of day;*
> *Rage, rage against the dying of the light.*
>   Dylan Thomas (d. 1953)

Dylan Thomas, himself, died way too early at the age of 39. But he didn't have to face old age where he pictured himself raving against the heavens at the close of day. That's a young man's imagination at work there picturing himself about how he would defy death in his old age (as if he were still young). Thomas was, I think, unrealistic in his poem, though heroic in spirit.

It wasn't his drinking apparently but pneumonia, the prescription of morphine (poorly prescribed) and finally sliding into a coma which caused Thomas to die. All his bluster, courage and rage against death did him no good; after all, at the end he was in a coma and he had no choice but "to go gently into that good night."

Maybe it's different when you're clear of mind but Kenny too slid into a coma in the last two days before he died so silently to slip away. We go through this world with so much vim and vigor when we are young but when things come to the end, then we are stooped and frail and call on God (or something) to help us.

My Brother-in-Law
Got Sick

> *This is the way the world ends:*
> *This is the way the world ends:*
> *This is the way the world ends:*
> ***Not** with **a bang** but **a whimper**.*
>   T.S. Elliot (d. 1965)

> *And you, my father, there on that sad height,*
> *Curse, bless, me now with your fierce tears, I pray.*
> *Do not go gentle into that good night.*
> *Rage, rage against the dying of the light.*
>   Dylan Thomas (d. 1953)

CHAPTER 24

Through those months from March 2007 to December 2007, Kenny journeyed through the stages of rage to hope and then to acceptance.   It was a metamorphosis involving agony at each stage. I wish I had his posts to share with the world...but I don't. My own weak memories and my frail insights will have to do to fill in the gaps.

The subtitle in Kenny's Blog was, *The Medical Mystery that is Me.* I want to go beyond the medical side and uncover the mystery that was essentially Kenny as an entire person.

It's a difficult pursuit, maybe a solitary one on my part, because the dynamics among family and friends have changed since Kenny died.

Everybody has gone their own way, and maybe memories are still too painful to exhume? Nobody wants that; nobody needs that! I'll do the best I can because what Kenny thought and felt during his illness should not be forgotten. It should be shared with others, as a tribute to his memory and what he thought about living and dying.

Dying is a lonely act and maybe all you have for comfort is sharing your thoughts and feelings with family and friends.   Kenny extended an open invitation when he got sick: "please feel free to drop by anytime over this coming weekend and beyond. We would love to see you!" We all need comforting words, "like a bridge over troubled waters".

AFTERNOON

It's turning out to be a beautiful afternoon. I just brought my basketball in after shooting hoops in the gym at the UM church. I'm glad it's only a 3 minute walk there.

The sun is beaming into our Great Room again today, shining through those Austrian crystals suspended from the triangular windows above the sliding doors, sprinkling little rainbows across the walls, across Kenny's paintings and also over the family photo album opened on the carpet.

Rainbows over the family photos? The human mind reads symbolism into such things and sees things that aren't really there but it's a nice thought anyway. Rainbows over the family photos! A lovely association. How promising!

I looked at today's list of little things to do (my wife's neat printing):

- Do the pomegranate
- Deposit cheque
- Mail Scholastic envelope
- Buy lemon

I've mailed the envelope and just finished doing the pomegranate after shooting hoops at the local church for exercise. Extricating the seeds out of a pomegranate is a messy business. I put on my work pants and took the knife and cutting board out to the back yard. Working on the pomegranate reminded me of mining red rubies out of all my writing about Kenny. I cut the pomegranate into slices and then with my fingers gingerly cracked open the slices and plucked out the individual kernels into a plastic container, so that Marjorie can have that for her cereal. The cutting board gets awfully bloody from the juice. Blood and little rubies. What a messy job but so worth it!

Well, it's almost time for *Peter Gunn* again. Henry Mancini's theme music is pretty cool! It's Tuesday and *NCIS* will also be on tonight, Marjorie's favourite crime show, on the digital Buffalo station, 4-1. I just love that theme music too, great stuff, good crime show!

> Out here in the fields
> I fight for my meals
> I get my back into my living
> I don't need to fight
> To prove I'm right
> I don't need to be forgiven
> > performed by Numeriklab
> > composed by Matt Hawkins,
> > Maurice Jackson & Neil Martin

Evenings usually mean good reception through out digital TV aerial but not always. So we're hoping for the best tonight.

I looked up at the sunbathed TV tower in the back yard after bringing in the pomegranate. My two antennas were glittering bright up there in the sun. Propitious?

Rainbows over family photos and shiny new aerials? Maybe that doesn't mean a thing but the mind does like to impose a good symbolic meaning on what the eyes see.

Rainbows and glitter mean a more promising and brighter side to life, don't they! We know that appearances can be deceiving. As to the glittering antennas: I still don't trust the Buffalo station because it fades in and out during the day. And as to our family photo dappled with pretty rainbows: we've lost Laura (Kenny's mother), Opa and Oma Boldt and Kenny most recently. They exist only in the picture and in the mind, but are no more.

Kenny was a cute little shaver in that family photo too, about 8 years of age, standing beside his mom and dad, with his hands cupped over the top of Oma's chair.

That was a visual memory of another time and day (maybe in another universe, our timeline hasn't given him cancer yet – maybe they are still alive?)

Rainbow streaks continue to dance over our family photo. Words can be deceiving too. Rainbows and glitter? It's all nice sounding stuff, but deep down we are sad!

*****

Oh well, it's time for lunch and the music for *Peter Gunn* is telling me to snap out of it!

I found a few insightful lines in today's episode, about a politician vying for the State Senate: his slogan was "representation without taxation," vote for Adrian Grimmett!   His campaign buttons read: Grow With Grimmett.

Somebody shot the campaign manager and tried to embezzle a million dollars worth of funds stashed in a trunk. Peter Gunn goes looking for the killer. He wants to buy information in a Japanese restaurant. (Don't ask!)

A gorgeous blonde is sitting on the floor and tugs at his pant trousers from behind a beaded curtain to get his attention. (You're supposed to sit on the floor in a Japanese restaurant?

How awkward!) The blonde is tipsy holding a martini glass in her hand.

"Oh, you're cute just like my fourth husband," she says. "That's nice," says Gunn. "Not really. He got run over by a train."

She wants him to have a drink with her because she is depressed and disenchanted with the whole world. "The whole world is in a smear!" She pronounces it, "shmear." Gunn asks her to explain. "Just look around, everything's a mess. The whole world's in a shmear." Gunn repartees: "If we all hold a good thought, it'll straighten itself out." Well, the blonde is not convinced: "Maybe yes, maybe no...but this'll help," she says, lifting her martini glass.

Gunn sees the manager and offers him a bribe for information. But the manager doesn't budge. "What's the matter, you don't want to see your business grow?" "Not by an explosion," remarks the manager. He mutters something in Japanese. "What's that mean?" questions Gunn. "Keep smiling Charlie Brown!"

Later when Lieutenant Jacoby and Gunn are together, having killed the killers and recovered the trunk full of money, they wonder about the strangeness of politics and if Grimmett would actually stand a chance getting into the State House with his slogan, "representation without taxation."

Jacoby says it's impossible; he'll never get in with that idea. Gunn counters: "Nothing's impossible, Lieutenant."

The camera focuses on their lapels. They are both wearing campaign buttons: Grow With Grimmett! Then the credits appear with that catchy Henry Mancini theme music. Ah, I just love it. Man, they could make great black and white films in those days! (vintage MCMLX)

Craig Stevens, by the way, who starred as the suave detective in the series, *Peter Gunn*, died of cancer in 2000 in Los Angeles at the age of 81. At least, he hit 81.

CHAPTER 25

The white clouds are now sailing across the blue skies like Spanish galleons on a windy sea. The sun is disappearing and it's calling for rain and grey clouds again later in the day. I hope I don't get a weather headache. I feel like I've actually started a real book. Maybe this seedling will grow.

The Canadian Writer's Market, 18th edition, arrived last Friday. I finally broke it out of its cardboard shipping box. I'll have to see what Joanna Karaplis has to say about marketing a potential book. But I will do that, maybe tomorrow. At least, it's another step for you, Kenny, to let people know your name. "If we all hold a good thought, it'll straighten itself out." (my hero, Peter Gunn 1960)

I thought my wife would come home really late tonight because of the staff meeting. She has to lesson plan afterwards and then she drives home in the dark. It's already getting dark by 5:00 p.m. now-a-days, so my wife is tired and usually down in spirits by the time she gets home. And here I am writing about *Peter Gunn*, about the billowing clouds like Spanish Galleons and about rainbows that play over the family photo.

She came home earlier than usual today though but still looked really tired and drawn out.

I took her coat, her lunch bag and school bags. I started the quinoa and the barbecue for our steaks. She commented, "This is a good supper." I'd hoped so because I need her to survive her long days in teaching, especially when she has a staff meeting after school. She settled in for the evening with her housecoat, her book (Lee Child *Bad Luck And Trouble*) and I told her to call me for that sitcom, *The Big Bang Theory* because we need a laugh or two. We'll move to the Great Room for *NCIS* right afterwards. *NCIS* is a show which intersperses humour amidst the crime solving plot.

The Big Bang Theory has become a favourite for us, like *Corner Gas* used to be. I'm glad we got the 32" TV and that I finished running those coaxial cables from the antennas into the crawlspace at the back of the house before the weather got too cold. The stress of life needs be broken up with holidays and entertainment.   I'll look at *The Canadian Writer's Market* tomorrow. Writing a book or selling it is not the making of one day! It's also something that doesn't appeal to my nature. "I'm a writer, not a salesman," as Bones, Doctor Leonard McCoy on Star Trek might say.

Somebody once said, (and I think it was me): "There's a book in everybody; it's just a matter of writing it down!"

Hopefully, the details will come out word by word as I stubbornly plug along and try to find "le mot juste." But that's easier said than done! Didn't the great sculptor, Michelangelo (d. 1564), say something similar? "The statue already exists inside the marble. All you have to do is free the idea inside from the superfluous matter surrounding it."

There's so much stuff running around in my mind, what do I include and what do I throw away?   Not every memory makes a book that's of value to the public.

Anyway, I still have to find a publisher who will put all my hard work into print, so others can see it. I've finally glanced at *The Canadian Writer's Market.* Now to send out feelers with a good query letter! And that is a lot of busy work too, sigh!

I've got another migraine and my eyesight is shimmering in front of me, twinkling lights, and my head hurts. The pharmacist did not recommend *Excedrin* because it has aspirin and codeine in it which contravenes with my daily coumadin, a blood thinner. I've got to lie down. I wish I had the health to just grab this book idea and chisel it out like Michelangelo's sculpted statue. Clouds are rolling in this afternoon making the sky look dull and white. I feel sleepy and headachy and need a lie-down. Rome was not built in a day.

CHAPTER 26

Lady Luck and Leukemia
November 23, 2010

All 29 miners have been saved in China; 29 miners have died after a second explosion in New Zealand. That averages out to 0, so nothing was gained except those 29 miners in China I'm sure had family members who were grateful. Sad about the other 29 in New Zealand!

North and South Korea are pointing guns at each other and an American Battleship is sailing into the Yellow Sea. Has anyone ever heard of the "Balkan Powder Keg" which sparked the First World War in 1914? Sarah Palin's book is making headlines: *America by Heart: Reflections on Family, Faith and Flag.* Her name on the cover is bigger than her title (I thought it was supposed to be the other way around?).

George W. Bush has a new book out too: *Decision Points.* Saen Higgins is pushing his new book, *Wealth Without Risk*, in infomercials on TV. He claims that people can get rich, "just get my book", "without having to punch a time clock", "simply can't lose." He apparently tells you how to buy houses cheaply and sell them for a fortune, to transform $993 into $196,000! The real estate term for this is "flipping." Then there's *Rich Dad, Poor Dad Seminars* by Robert J. Kiyosaki.

And here I am trying to light a little candle for Kenny in the printed word. I feel so small. Will the world ever see the flicker of Kenny's little candle with all the other noise that's going on in the world? Thank you, Darriane for lighting a remembrance candle for your daddy at church last Sunday.

Marjorie asked me to put $40 into her lunch bag. The school staff pooled money together for Lottery 649 which is supposed to be up to 25 million dollars this week. Marjorie prefers not to enter things like that, but it's supposed to be the sociable thing to do, to participate. Meantime, Haiti is struggling with a cholera outbreak after their 7.0 magnitude earthquake 10 months ago (and you wonder what's been done there in all this time?)

November 24, 2010
It came in the mail. I think it was spring 2003. A manila envelope from the Juravinski Cancer Clinic in Hamilton. I was shocked.

Just a few weeks prior, I'd gone to the Beamsville Clinic for my routine blood check, my INR, to make sure that the thinning in my blood was within acceptable parameters for my artificial aortic heart valve which I had acquired back in 1987. I'm on 2 mg of coumadin daily to keep plaque off it.

My family physician did not call me back about the results to my INR. That was strange, usually I get a phone call, so I assumed everything was A-okay. And here I receive this manila envelope in the mail. I opened it and looked at a booklet on cancer support and contacts, with paperwork on a date and time for an appointment at the Juravinski. I made an appointment with my family physician in Beamsville and expressed my concern that he did not let me know first.

I found out that my white blood cell count was higher than normal (10 being normal and mine was at 12) and so the paperwork went ahead to put me into the system (except they neglected to include the personal element where the family physician tells you personally, instead of sending you a manila envelope in the mail).

I kept this news from Marjorie for several days and then, not sleeping at nights, I finally told her in the middle of the night: "I have something to tell you." She said, she loved me and that we'd be in this together. She came with me to that appointment at the Juravinski in Hamilton.

The lady doctor told us: "If there is any kind of cancer you'd want, it's this one."

She said that people can go for years with chronic leukemia without it going into the acute stage. I would have preferred not to have had the problem at all!

I had to come back to the Juravinski every 3 months for a year and if clear, then I'd have yearly check-ups. That's the way it's been for 7 years now. My last level was 14.9. I was told that I don't have to worry about treatment until the count goes up to 20.

I don't like these little yearly increments that keep creeping up and up towards 20 but I can't do anything about it. I wish I were on Star-Trek's *U.S.S. Enterprise* [The Next Generation] where Beverley Crusher can just wave an electronic wand to bring my blood levels back to normal.

I feel like a ticking time bomb. It was scary to have this sentence pronounced on me the first time I heard it in 2003, especially the manner in which it was communicated to me with a manila envelope by mail.

However, unlike Kenny, I was not told, "You have only a few months to live." I suppose, in the big scheme of things, the world would not miss either one of us, except for immediate family and friends. We take it for granted to be healthy and to continue with daily life like normal with no worries, except the usual hum-drum stress of daily living.

I didn't mention my leukemia in the Blog when Kenny launched it in the spring of 2007. Kenny was the immediate worry.

However, fate throws complications our way. I was seriously sidelined with gout that late spring which put me in a wheelchair. With Kenny and then with me, the family had way more than they could handle. The Universe or God targeted us with worries on overload!

Kenny did not know about my leukemia situation until the end of May 2007 when I sent him a separate and private email outside of the Blog informing him of my situation since 2003. I did not think it was appropriate to let people in general know about my leukemia on the Blog. With the gout putting me in a wheelchair, I wanted to share my story about leukemia as well, because now Kenny and I were comrades in arms, each personally involved with that word, cancer.

I guess there's a need in people to share secrets and to complain about ailments too. What good is suffering if you can't share, and even better, what good if you can't complain about it!

From: John Hartig
To: Ken Janzen
Sent: May 31, 2007
Subject: sharing my story

Ken:

I'm not sure if this is fit for the Blog *'cause it's just more bitchin'* *'bout the system* ... but this time, from my personal experience.

Four years ago, I received an envelope in the mail from the *Juravinski Cancer Centre* at the Henderson Hospital. I had an appointment to check leukemia.

"Holy crap! I've got leukemia?" nobody told me about that! That week, I made an appointment with my family doctor who told me my last blood count showed a high level of white blood cells. (I get monthly blood checkups anyway for my INR or blood thinning since I'm on coumadin -- necessary for my artificial heart valve.)

The family doctor just left me out of the loop in arranging this appointment for me with the higher ups, who just mailed me directly.

I hid that letter from Marjorie for like 3 days, worrying and not sleeping in the meantime. Then one night while in bed in the dark, I just plain told her, "I've got leukemia." We talked about it and opening up to her was the best thing I could have done, spiritually and psychologically.

She took a day off school and we both drove to Hamilton for the specialist's appointment. I had to get pricked by the needle for blood samples before I saw the cancer specialist.

Within the hour, the specialist called me in: "Of the cancers you could have, this is the best kind!"

It was not "acute leukemia", it was "chronic leukemia" -- which is leukemia that just hasn't broken out yet -- and could remain at a low level for 10, 15...or an undetermined number of years.

I don't know that I was really reassured about this "good news" though, that it was "the best kind of cancer possible to get" -- how nice -- I would prefer no cancer at all, of any kind, if you please! I'm sure you know how these feelings go, Ken.

Now, I'm scheduled at the Juravinski Clinic for yearly checkups. The doctor also said: "The main thing is that we got you into the system."

I'm wondering though what kind of system we'll have when "the forces that be" replace our formerly universal health care system with two-tiered health care.

Twenty years ago our health care system was touted as the envy of the world. We've taken so much for granted. And we are turning a blind eye or taking it too quietly with all these cutbacks and changes while politicians vote themselves a 30% wage hike.

My main point: I couldn't believe getting that letter in the mail four years ago. Hey there, medical profession! Don't leave me out of the loop...I'm here! God knows I'm here!

John

PS: If you think it appropriate, Ken, you can slip this into the Blog for me. I wanted to clear it with you first because I didn't know how long my rant would be or whether you thought it appropriate for your Blog. Also my wife, your sister, is so protective of you, she doesn't want me to send these complaints to your Blog. She's perfectly right.

I'd like you to know my story. Now that you know: Please delete this missive...because I don't think it will self-destruct in 10 seconds.

PPS: Love ya.

CHAPTER 27

Back to the Future
November 24, 2010

It would be ironic if this book is the Universe's way of giving us a second chance at telling Kenny's little story, actually a double story about him and me!

I hope it's not my own requiem, where I might die, if and after this work gets published. I don't want this thing to be a parallel to Kenny's Blog and his fate. We've had enough misfortune in the family! I'd like more years to play with Braeden and Darriane, Kenny's little ones, because my wife and I can't have kids of our own. I like visiting Marilyn's grand-kids, Ethan and Liam, when they come over to grandma's house, so I can get a chance to play with them too.

The cards that fate has dealt a person are loaded with a mix of luck and fate. But a lot also rides on how you play the hand.

I'm thinking back almost 3 weeks and the announcement that the Oscar nominated actress, Jill Clayburgh, died of chronic leukemia on November 6, 2010 at the age of 66. She'd been "carrying" the disease for 21 years and nobody knew about it. I remember how touched I was by her performance in "An Unmarried Woman." Having gone through a traumatic breakup myself some years ago, I remember how soul ripping that experience was. Jill Clayburgh was a courageous person.

The main thing I've gotten out of marriage to Marjorie, over the past 23 years, is my sense of belonging. If you've noticed by now, I hardly ever use her name in this writing. She hates the internet and is protective of her anonymity. Anyway, I've been accepted by her, "adopted" by the Janzen family and made new as a person with a new purpose in life, after, I confess, two nervous break-downs.

> *I was lost on an endless sea*
> *Going down, going down, going down on an endless sea*
> *Sail with the wind, you weather the storm*
> *You bring it all home, bring it all home, you bring it all home*
> > (Gerry Rafferty 1978)
> > > (born 16 April 1947;
> > > died 4 January 2011 liver failure)

November 25, 2010
MORNING
Today, I heard on the radio that CARP (Canadian Association of Retired Persons) announced that there will be more people over 65 slipping into poverty. Oh joy! I'm 64 and in approximately 3 months, I will hit 65.

I recently got my pension statement from Ontario Teachers and my annual stipend from my teaching career will be a whopping $13,000 per year. I get just under $500 from my Old Age Pension (which is another $6,000 per year) and that gives me a grand total of $19,000 a year to live on (before taxes).

If I were single, that means I'd be just a shave over the poverty limit, according to the 2009 stats: $16,245.00 /annual$ 7.81/hour. My goodness, where did I miss the boat? -- with an M.A. in English Literature and a Teaching Degree? I taught in the Christian School System for a number of years and that didn't help my pension any because there are no benefits. Then two nervous breakdowns didn't help either. I got them as a teacher because I wanted to teach the subject, which kids weren't interested in, and I just was no good at discipline, what they call euphemistically, "classroom management". I asked for help from the office, and found out the office didn't want to hear about it, and expected you to sink or swim. I sunk..twice, and should have realized that teaching was not for me. But that's another story.

I took myself out of the work force (not finding work) to go to school in several attempts to reboot myself into another career (which failed).

So here I am facing a pittance for my pension in what was my life's contribution to society. Somehow I missed the boat and society missed the boat on me. I appreciate more than ever what Kenny went through as a self-employed individual striving to make a living and to support his family financially. I'm just lucky I'm covered under Marjorie's teacher insurance plan for dental and drug needs.

EVENING
Oprah made some interesting points on TV. This is her last year on the TV talk show (however will the American society do without her?) She's reviewed salient points in her career, one of them being the death of John F. Kennedy Junior who died in a plane crash at the age of 38 (July 16, 1999). His wife, Carolyn Bessette, and sister-in-law, Lauren Bessette, were also killed in the light aircraft, a Piper Saratoga, which John F. was piloting. The

trio was apparently headed to Martha's Vineyard for a wedding, a happy occasion.

Oprah summed up John F.'s death this way: "He is forever handsome, promising, frozen in time." I guess the same could be said of many people who die too young, including Kenny.

Oprah also told a little story about a cashmere scarf. A friend got it as a gift and it was so expensive and so pretty, that the person went to the store to get a cheaper one to wear, so the other one could be stored safely away. In the process of going to stores, looking for a replacement, this person lost the original cashmere scarf. Moral of the story: "Wear it now! Enjoy it!" I guess relationships are that way too. Cherish near ones and dear ones while you have them.

Marjorie came home early enough, so we could get to that blue grass gospel concert downtown for which we paid $40. *House of Doc* from Winnipeg was featured, all talented Mennonite people, fiddle, guitar, banjo, accordian and drum.

I told Marjorie not to go to her seminar after school but to finish her lesson plan for the next day and just head home...because we had a life! The "theater" was set up like a beatnik coffee house, little tables and candles lit in the center. Percolating coffee on a side counter. We sat near the back by the window. It was raining outside. The group sang a song by Warren Zevon who died of terminal lung cancer in 2003 at the age of 56:

Shadows are falling and I'm running out of breath
Keep me in your heart for awhile
If I leave you it doesn't mean I love you any less
Keep me in your heart for awhile

> *When you get up in the morning and you see that crazy sun*
> *Keep me in your heart for while...*
> *Hold me in your thoughts, take me to your dreams*
> *Touch me as I fall into view*
> *When the winter comes keep the fires lit*
> *And I will be right next to you...*
>   (Warren Zevon 2003)

My wife sobbed. She thought of Kenny. I held her. Over the past 3 years, she's often said to me: "I miss Kenny so much!" "Love ya Guys, Kenny!" —signed cover on his CD. Wikipedia says that the singer/songwriter, Warren Zevon, was: "a man who retained his mordant sense of humor, even as his health was deteriorating over time."

I'm reminded of the words in another song:

> *But for the grace of God go I*
> *I must've been born a lucky guy*
> *Heaven only knows how I've been blessed*
> *With the gift of your love...*
>   (country singer, Keith Urban b. 1967)

Marjorie and I walked back to our car in the rain. As soon as we got home, I recorded *The Mentalist,* our second favourite crime show, next to *NCIS.* We listened to the rain pitter-pattering on the roof as we tried to sleep. Sleep comes hard now-a-days and we each take a Melatonin each night to help us slip into slumber.

Marjorie woke up with a terrible sinus attack. This is usually triggered by some sort of scent she's encountered during the day and doesn't always manifest itself right away. She feels like she's drowning with her sinuses draining into the back of her throat. Her life would be so much easier if she didn't have that problem and if she could only sleep. If only?   "It's really bad tonight?" I asked.   Marjorie responded: "I think it was the candles at the concert. They must have been scented?" "Doesn't bother anybody else!" I said, "But those are the people that don't think about the few who might be affected."

There needs to be more awareness about effects of perfume and scented candles in public places, just like smoking.   Scent free! Smoke free!

CHAPTER 28

The 13th Precinct
Friday, November 26, 2010

AFTERNOON
Thank goodness that Peter Gunn has Lieutenant Jacoby, from the 13th precinct, as a friend! Jacoby loves to read *The Financial Review* but he's no slouch when it comes to using a gun. He's saved Gunn's bacon a couple of times in the series.

This particular episode is about a mentally unbalanced former jockey who was injured by a horse and the jockey is out to get revenge in a plan to kill the horse. So we've got a pile of bookies, jockeys, circus people, detectives, thugs and the police in this well crafted story.

I loved the scene where Gunn is hired to find out who killed the horse's trainer. Gunn listens to his client and leans back leisurely listening and holding a cigarette. His suit and tie are as neat and tidy as a pin, like James Bond's attire.

Next scene, Gunn is talking ethics with a bookie, named Scooter. The bookie has information on Russo, the suspect, the police are looking for. But it's not him; it's the jockey! Scooter picks up the first telephone call and gives the caller a tip that so and so will win in the fifth. Scooter tells Gunn where to find Russo. Scooter picks up the second phone call and gives the caller a tip that some other so and so will win in the fifth. Gunn asks him how two different horses can win in the same race?   Gunn remarks:

"You're selling every horse in the race!" Scooter justifies himself, in an evidently Yiddish accent, that the losers lose but the winners win, but hey, they really love him! "A man should want everyone to like him, otherwise he's insecure," he comments.

Next scene, Gunn finds Russo's hideout (information from the bookie, it's a setup). Russon declares his innocence, Gunn is inclined to believe him. He meets the innocent crook in what looks like a warehouse, with boxes piled high that say, Handle With Care. The sleazy scenes are accompanied by low key background jazz music with a beatnik beat: xylophone and double bass, plucked. Cool Henry Mancini!

Next scene, Gunn gets waylaid in his own apartment by a huge man, "big as an elephant," but Gunn's suit never gets ruffled. Reminds you of James Bond before James Bond became an icon? Jacoby breaks into the apartment just in time and the giant flees.

Next scene, Gunn meets Jack LaLanne on set. Jack looks trim like a V and plugs in a promo for his exercise show on TV. He and Gunn are friends and Jack gives gives a little health advice: "If they look better, they'll feel better. I'm trying to get people to exercise."

Gunn asks him if he ever trained anybody who was huge and had a scar on his cheek. LaLanne trained anything from wrestlers to circus actors. He pinpoints the guy and tells Gunn, yes, he knew the man but "the man had nothing upstairs."

Jack LaLanne was a pioneer creating a demand in a field of work where the phrase, "personal trainer," hadn't come into vogue yet.

He lets Gunn know how to get a hold of the crazy jockey and the ungentle giant, who are both killed in the end as the bad guys.

The giant is shot by Jacoby before Gunn is thrown across the room in a wrestling airplane spin. The jockey holds up a gun to the horse in the stable but can't fire because his hands have previously been maimed by that same horse 2 years back (which ended the jockey's career).

The shot is poorly aimed and the horse kicks the jockey in the head. Jacoby remarks: "He's dead." Gunn replies: "He's been dead twice, the first time 2 years ago." Henry Mancini music kicks in. Credits role.
These bad guys not only are bad shots but they never learn! And often they get caught in the end by talking too much when they hold a gun, except in this case, when they get shot or are kicked in the head by a horse.

I had a point in this, actually several, but what was it? Hmmm.

The giant had no brains and apparently couldn't hold down a job. He mixed with poor company just because he thought the jockey was his friend. The jockey had brains and didn't have the imagination to find a second career, so he had to "die twice."

LaLanne was a small guy too but had talent to create a TV show on physical fitness way back in the 1950s. He said that as a boy he was hooked on sugar and junk food until he was 15.

LaLanne blames overly-processed foods for many health problems. He advocates a vegetarian diet, though he eats some fish himself, and has described organic food as "a bunch of bull."

He is a Doctor of Chiropractic and a fitness expert. A physical trainer before his time! Born: 1914!

At this point, in 2010, Jack LaLanne is 96 years old and still very active promoting a healthy diet and juicing. Craig Stevens, alias Peter Gunn, died in 2000 of cancer at the age of 81. Maybe the luck of the draw gives you health and brains but surely those bad guys in this *Peter Gunn* episode could have made better choices in their lives, even if life put them behind the 8 ball!

> *I'd unravel every riddle for any individ'le,*
> *In trouble or in pain.*
> *With the thoughts you'll be thinkin'*
> *you could be another Lincoln*
> *If you only had a brain.*
>   (Scarecrow, Wizard of Oz, 1939)

By the way, if the villains in that *Peter Gunn* episode didn't have brains, then they should have worked on their courage or heart to make this world a better place! Kenny had all three. When he was going through his cancer, dad proudly mentioned "the mettle" Kenny was made of.

It's time to make chili. It tastes better if it sits. Andrew's baptism is coming this Sunday and I promised to bring my world famous chili. The guys in Teen Challenge will appreciate it. Now to work! Dad is making his world famous borscht, so the guys definitely won't be underfed!

Young people should google Jack LaLanne and certainly watch the 1939 version of the *Wizard of Oz*.

CHAPTER 29

Time for a Change
Saturday, November 27, 2010

A change of season in Canada means a change of tires. Usually that's November. My wife needed snow tires for her drive to school this winter, getting to Smith School off Oakes Rd. by way of the QEW highway. We got stuck on a side road one year taking Darriane back home, had to abandon the car and drudge through a blizzard and a foot deep snow to get to Kenny's house. We weren't going through that again, not with my wife's lame ankle and need of a cane.

I picked Jerry up, my brother-in-law, and we drove out to the town's maintenance yard where he works during the week. One of the perks of the job is that he gets to use some of the equipment there on Saturday morning on his day off.

The wind was very chilly and changing tires would be more comfortable inside the garage. When we finished, a few flakes of snow were already blowing down from a very grey sky. We drove home on the service road, past a graveyard in Grimsby and Jerry looked at the spots where town workers were preparing two new graves. I mentioned how my wife was still missing Kenny after 3 years. I wondered how cities and towns could find plots with all the people over the years that must be buried in cemeteries. Cremation has helped since the town allows you to stack 4 urns into one plot now-a-days.   We drove along Hwy 8 past the cemetery where Kenny was buried and my thoughts hovered over memories of him.

"He must be so cold in the ground," I remarked. "That's not him," Jerry said. I commented that they could throw my ashes over *Ball's Falls* for all I cared. It would save the family money.

I had been to Kenny's grave at least a dozen times over the past 3 years, mostly bicycling in and putting the bike down beside the grave. I walked in a couple of times and even wrote a poem, one snowy winter day, about visiting Kenny's grave shortly after he died. I found no answers and I heard no God whisper to me. God was silent.

Only Kenny's grey gravestone stared back at me:
"Loving Husband, Father and Son. Kenneth Wayne "Ken" Janzen August 5, 1970 January 18, 2008   You lived for those you loved and those you loved remember."

A treble clef, a few notes and keyboard ivories adorn the stone.

*****

I guess God isn't supposed to be a wish list when you pray. That's human imagination. God should be something more than a miracle worker for humans to make things go right. That would be a paltry image of God, made in the image of man.

But most of us humans are like that, wanting God to do our bidding and singing his praises when things do go our way. I usually hold my tongue when I hear someone praise the Lord because something nice happened to them.

That kind of thinking is exemplified in that football game (Nov. 2010) where the Steelers edged out the Buffalo Bills 19-16 after "Stevie" Johnson fumbled the football in what should have been the winning touchdown for Buffalo.

Johnson blamed God publicly on twitter: *"I PRAISE YOU 24/7!!!!!! AND THIS HOW YOU DO ME!!!!! YOU EXPECT ME TO LEARN FROM THIS??? HOW???!!! ILL NEVER FORGET THIS!! EVER!!! THX THO..."*

How sarcastic towards God!

Ruth Manuel-Logan, reporter for the *Black Voices On Sports* web site, wrote that a lot of people were plain peeved at Stevie Johnson. She put a relationship to God in this perspective: "Hey, Stevie, let me pull your coattails, God has his hands pretty full right about now than to concern himself with a mere football game. Save your pleas for more important matters and handle your consequences like an adult."

But people are people when it comes to human understanding and human needs. I agree that God shouldn't cater to us in a trade-off, if you do this for me, God, I will praise You!

I feel uncomfortable when I see sports figures cross themselves when they score, not that a belief in God itself makes me uncomfortable, just that people seem to reduce God to a servant who manipulates the outcome of a game in their favour.

Nations do the same, when they go to war, and they chant that God is on their side! How stupidly presumptuous!

And yet, we prayed for Kenny in what was more important than a mere football game; it was a life and death struggle and still Kenny died and still we did not understand why God allowed it. We hold on to faith anyway...well, because we simply have to. The world is so full of chaos; faith helps us through.

I don't care about intellectual suicide if you believe in God. I confess to a need to believe in an Almighty Being who cares about me personally. There is so much tragedy in the world.

My nervous breakdown in 1984 bottomed me out and whether it was a false hope or not, the Bible was something I clung to my bosom for sanity.

Kenny read the Bible in his last few months from October to December 2007. Pastor Henry Wiebe told Kenny to read the *Psalms* of David, particularly this one, Psalm 139:

> *All the days ordained for me*
> *Were written in our book*
> *Before one of them came to be.*
>   (Psalm 139: v.16)

Even while Kenny's body was slowly dying through November and December and finally through January, his spirit was going through a rebirth. He told his wife and sisters that he wanted his kids to be raised as Christians.

CHAPTER 30

Introducing Andrew
Sunday, November 28, 2010

My nephew (and Kenny's nephew), Andrew, experienced a rebirth today. I photographed his baptism at St. Ann's Community Church. Andrew wanted to make this a special occasion for himself and his family since he was turning his life around. Andrew was jailed for theft some months back when he needed money to support a drug habit of speed and cocaine. He is 24 now and in rehab in London, Ontario, in a program called *Teen Challenge*.

His parents and Andrew's lawyer influenced the judge that rehabilitation through *Teen Challenge* would be a better choice for Andrew than prison.

Teen Challenge is a boot camp with strict rules, funded by public and private donations, with the aim of redirecting law breakers into decent citizens with Christian based lives. *Teen Challenge* is located on what used to be farm land and houses several dorms, kitchen and cafeteria facilities and a huge garage where "inmates" can repair cars and maintain the equipment necessary to keep the grounds in good shape. The rules are tough: no girlfriends, visits only certain times of the month, no communication except only certain times a month and of course, attendance at church services.

Andrew wanted to leave his drugs behind and become a mentor to others who had lost their way. He volunteered for the Salvation

Army soup kitchen and three rough looking guys said he knew nothing about the stuff they were going through. Andrew said that he knew exactly what they were going through. He'd been there with the drugs. One of the fellows wanted to know how to get into *Teen Challenge* and that's how Andrew was selected as being a mentor for people wanting to leave a life of drugs behind.

Andrew looked at baptism as a rebirth and at *Teen Challenge* as the helping hand for a new beginning. He had been accepted into the *Teen Challenge* choir some months previously. He went on tour with them, accepted not only for his singing voice but also for his ability as a drummer. The choir did the entire worship service at St. Ann's Community Church (Andrew's home church) for Andrew's baptism there.

This rag-tag bunch, social failures and criminals, were now clean and the members of their choir were ambassadors for *Teen Challenge* traveling throughout Ontario to different churches to raise funds to help pay the bills to keep the London facility going.

The guitarist was a large chunk of a man in his 20s who had tattoos up and down his arm. On his knuckles were the words, on the right hand, in capital letters, STAY, and on the left, DOWN. He had been the "enforcer" in a gang that collected money from drug addicts. When bills needed collecting, this man (also named Andrew) was sent out to "encourage" payment.

After the choir's performance, the congregation retired to the old sanctuary where Andrew was baptized. He gave his testimony unabashedly while his parents, uncles and aunts and grandpa Wally listened to a confession about his addiction to heroine and cocaine and drug dealing. Much of the family didn't even know about this. Jerry, his father, dunked Andrew in the baptismal water symbolizing his rebirth to a new life.

*Therefore, if anyone is in Christ, he is a new creation;
the old is gone, the new has come.*

Andrew wants to go to Bible College or to Culinary School. He has the makings of a great chef, as well as a singer, if his passion inclines him in those directions.
The church fed the group in a pot-luck lunch afterwards. I made a pot of chili and dad brought his famous borscht. Both chili and borscht vanished in no time.

Kenny and Andrew had several things in common. They were both very willful and were both good singers.

There was a time when Kenny couldn't stand living at home after high-school and his sister, Marilyn and husband Jerry, took him in under their roof. When Andrew went through a similar rebellious streak (ironically) against Marilyn and Jerry, it was Kenny (being married by then) who took Andrew into his house.

Kenny encouraged Andrew in his singing and the two of them recorded a very lovely tune that Kenny wrote for Andrew's older brother's wedding, Shaun and Rachel. Shaun and Rachel now have two little boys, Liam and Ethan, as cute as buttons. They are sure signs that time really flies and that these little guys will eventually grow into men in their own right.

Andrew dotes on his little cousins and gives them a thrill tossing them into the air with his 6'4" frame. How the wheel of life goes 'round and 'round!

So, on Sunday, Andrew took the symbolic dip for remaking his life. We know that God is bigger than a grocery list. We know that

Andrew has the talent, the courage and the manhood to find a better path for his life.

Tuesday, November 30, 2010
Today, November 30th, is the Feast Day of St. Andrew whose name comes from the Greek "andreia" which means manhood or valor. St. Andrew is commonly known as the patron saint of Scotland but is also recognized as a saint in Greece, Romania and Russia. He is the apostle who was crucified on a cross in the shape of an X in what is now Greece, not nailed but bound to prolong his suffering.

This is the commentary I found on the history of Saint Andrew: "He lived up to his name and demonstrated true Christian manhood and valor to the bitter end. We all still remember him two thousand years later, but how many remember his crucifier Aegeas?"   (2 Cor. 5:17)

People need to have hope and a chance to change their lives. Our Andrew seized that chance in his baptism on Sunday, November 28, 2010. There are dates worthwhile remembering where you make a crucial turn in life. There are also people worthwhile remembering, how they lived and how they died.

For Andrew, for the rest of the family and for his friends, Kenny's life and death held crucial memories that, I hope, will make us all better human beings. Kenny's story needs the telling in this cagey crazy world of ours.

CHAPTER 31

It's a Cagey Crazy World
Monday, November 29, 2010

We woke up at 5:45 a.m. to a Haydn concerto introduced on FM 96.3 by Mike Duncan and Jean Stilwell. How can anybody be that energetic in the early morning and have a right to be that perky? I told my wife, "Mike Duncan makes me sick!" Witty, wide-awake and taking the world by a verbal storm: Mike Duncan, a whirlwind wonder, radio announcer par excellence, whose perky parlance comes off the top of his head, with a fount of facts and quick trivia for radio listeners.

I can hardly crawl out of bed. My wife has had a bad night with 6 hot flashes and lots of throat draining. She has to face Monday and the start of another week at school. Yet, I'd say, she teaches better than most teachers throughout the day and has an excellent handle on classroom management and rapport with the kids.

FM 96.3 is my favourite radio station: "Beautiful music for a crazy world!" Great slogan. The guy or gal who thought that one up is a genius and hopefully was paid lots of money for that slogan.

The slogan recognizes the Yin and Yang of existence. The beauty and the ugliness. And how beauty offsets the terribleness of the ugliness.

I've noticed though lately [flashing forward to my radio listening in 2019] that the new host of "The Oasis", Mark Wigmore, has changed the wording a bit to "beautiful music for the world" in his announcements. This new phrasing ignores the other half, that the world is indeed a crazy place. By not saying it, does that somehow make the craziness disappear and make the world a better place by not admitting to the other half?

I've also heard Mark announce, "We've got the greatest music in the world for you!" These new slogans sound bland compared to the old one: "Beautiful music for a crazy world!"

The old slogan has a lot of "pizzazz" and tells the truth about this old world! I'd like to see FM 96.3 keep it. It's genius!

*****

I took the pomegranate out to the backyard this morning, to slice it up and clean it on the cutting board. It makes a mess indoors. Still dark outside. I turned on the back light. Frost on the plastic chair, so I carried the little pillow out with me. After Marjorie is gone, my chores will include: hand laundry, shirts and bras, and baking banana bread. A house-husband's work is never done! Am I a liberated man? The question doesn't even apply. It's my job to pitch in, period! She's got the job that pays the bills and I don't. Since my nervous breakdown, this is my job now in this relationship, as a "house-husband".

I know that Kenny, my dead brother-in-law, did the cooking at his place. That's simply because he could. He also did carpentry work. Well, I rewired much of the house, simply because I could and I had the time, since I don't go to a regular job anymore. There's so much that should not be stereotyped, although I might be labeled by some as a "house-husband." Sometimes though, the career thing does tug at the back of my mind.

Today's *Peter Gunn* episode was about talent again. A young rock singer was becoming a star, with a fake talent, promoted by a crooked agent who rigged the kid's guitar with an electronic gizmo that made him sound good. His agent murdered the hat check girl because the singer fell in love with her and she interfered with the agent's "meal ticket" to a lucrative future. I couldn't help but notice Gunn's cufflinks. Men wore them in those days in the 50s to display a taste of style on their dress shirts. Gunn offered the agent a cigarette. They both lit up and Gunn blew cigarette smoke out of both nostrils. That was also "cool" in those days, and presented an image of assurance and confidence.

In a later scene, the suave private investigator popped out of the back seat of a taxi cab and slipped a bill to the cabbie for information. The cab driver observed: "The whole world's cagey...crazy." I've often wondered what the world would be like if more people took music lessons and studied the arts? But even peaceful and artistic pursuits are no guarantee for keeping violence out of the human heart. People are led astray by greed, jealousy and ambition at all levels and that's why the world is "cagey and crazy."

The musician in that *Peter Gunn* episode rode to fame on false talent and the agent murdered an innocent girl who stood in the way of his greed. The agent resented his protégé for riding to the top of the charts on his managerial skill and brains. Talent wasn't the real thing that counted though; it was courage and heart in both the agent and his protégé, a thing neither of them had.

The world is cagey and crazy. I watch *Peter Gunn*, not only because it's old time entertainment, but also because it's my way of holding onto sanity, while the whole world seems to go crazy, or to hell in a hand basket, as some people might put it.

North and South Korea are still squaring off (and they are supposed to be the same race!) The world stage has had another ember thrown under it by WikiLeaks founder, Julian Assange, who released information on his purported gossip web site from secret papers kept by the United States on foreign backdoor dealings. The Saudis apparently wanted the U.S. to attack Iran, to "cut off the head of the snake." Hillary Clinton called this kind of leakage of private papers, irresponsible and inflammatory, not conducive to private debate among diplomats.

Jonathan Swift's satire comes to mind here in Gulliver's Voyage to Lilliput (publ. 1726). A professor has a suggestion for settling political differences (chapter VI). You take 100 leaders from opposite sides, choosing the ones with the closest matching craniums. You cut off their heads and exchange half the brain with the other. Of course, the work would have to require some exactness, says Swift. The professor argues: "that the two half brains being left to debate the matter between themselves within the space of one skull, would soon come to a good understanding."

Countries and religions can be so intractable in their views, that only death may be their final solution and of course, that final solution is ludicrous. Swift was a master of satire. Al-Qaeda, unfortunately, sees cutting off heads as a perfect solution for infidels. What a world we have inherited! And we thought we left Hitler and all that mess behind us in 1945!

Canada, of course, fared like its usual self in these WikiLeaks. It's been labeled as a country with "an inferiority complex." Jim Judd, former head of Canada's spy service, CSIS, was quoted as saying (in 2008) that Canadians have an "Alice In Wonderland" attitude toward global terrorism, that they are naïve and that the video of Omar Khadr's interrogation at Guantanamo Bay, Cuba, would trigger "knee-jerk anti-Americanism" and "paroxysms of moral outrage, a Canadian specialty." And indeed, it did just that!

What a bleeding heart country! And here, somebody like Clifford Olson has the right to collect old age pension cheques in jail after murdering 11 kids in British Columbia and then is eligible for parole in 2010. Well, one doesn't wonder about Canada being painted with an Alice In Wonderland brush.

Al-Qaeda, on the other hand is definite. They would side with the Queen of Hearts and decree: "Off with their heads!" Really, Canada doesn't need to be extreme but it needs to define itself more, with more definite laws and immigration policies. We've been so nice to everybody that terrorists have used us as a backdoor into the United States. I used to joke that Canada would never go to war unless *Tim Hortons* was at the front...and indeed that is exactly what's happened in Afghanistan. A newspaper headline read: *Tim Hortons has brought a taste of home to the troops in Kandahar.*

Meantime, the Kardashian sisters appeared on the talk-show, *The View*, today (November 29, 2010) to promote their autobiography: *Kardashian, Konfidential.* It's a tell-all book about their lives, the sex scandals and their reality show, *Keeping Up With the Kardashians.* All three sisters, Kourtney, Kim and Khloé, wore tight skirts and talked about tidbits that are buzz-worthy in their new autobiography. I consider this a sure sign of the vacuous value system stirred up by Hollywood and the paparazzi in American society and something that the Muslim world would point to (and rightly so) with derision.

CHAPTER 32

Retro TV & Commercials

I broke for lunch and later clicked to Retro TV, to watch the credits roll by on *The Rifleman* (1962) and then commercials that tell of a fractured U.S. society.

The Reverse Mortgage concept gives you money now to enjoy your life if you are 65 or older. Sounds great but the reality is that it's an idea that takes away your house before you die, where you sell your ownership "with this reverse idea", so you can spend money now and of course, your kids won't inherit a thing. Well, maybe that's not a bad idea, who knows?

Then there's Memory Flow where you get a 14 day free trial go give you a razor sharp memory. Hmmm. I could use that! Everybody knows you lose your memory as you get older. This will restore it! These ad people know how to throw out a "hook". They give you the first 14 days free. What they don't say is that once they've got you, you have to start paying, often with automatic renewals…and so they get a customer out of you. "The phone lines are open now!"

Get what you deserve! There's this drug that cures; this lawsuit that fights for you; this health-plan that covers you, no medical exam necessary.

Christmas is coming and Black Friday is just over; now we have Cyber Monday with online deals if you have your credit card handy. The almighty credit card, plastic money! It'll get you anything without the inconvenience of cash; it's invisible money and it feels like it's free.

Extremist Muslims must be laughing up their sleeves and saying, yes, there, you see how corrupt Western society is! The cab driver in that *Peter Gunn* episode had a real epiphany when he said: "The whole world's cagey...crazy." Maybe it wasn't so profound (nothing new under the sun) but it was the truth!

That nutty global macrocosm must have been just as crazy 3 years ago, when my brother-in-law, Kenny, was still alive and the family was focused on the microcosm of his suffering. Our private world of pain was so intense and so small then. Kenny closed the door to the outside world, as he closed the accounts of his website customers one by one, and had to tell them to go elsewhere for their business.

That November and December in 2007 were full of headlines about Climate Change, El Nino, Global Warming and of course, road-side bombings.

"Using satellite images, scientists found that Hurricane Katrina destroyed 5 million acres of trees across Mississippi and Alabama, and experts said it would take decades for the plant life to recover and some areas may be permanently damaged."

Al-Qaida made a headline in late December. It apparently targeted the Knights of Malta as a surviving remnant of the Christian crusades. In Afghanistan, by November 2007, a total of 73 Canadians had been killed, mostly by road side bombs. By the time Kenny died, on January 18, 2008, a total of 77 Canadians had been killed over there, and then another one was added only 5 days later.

All of these young men gone to graves everyone: 26, 25, 23 years of age! All of this was happening while Kenny was fighting his own private war with cancer, an internal war, like a roadside bomb that was so unfair. As of November 29, 2010, a total of 153 Canadians have traveled the highway of heroes to their funerals. Not only is weather vengeful but people add to the overall craziness on this planet. When will people ever learn, when will they stop, so we can deal with climate change and better health care, instead of the craziness of shooting each other?

One of the top 10 movies of 2007 was *The Bourne Ultimatum* and Kenny would have loved this action packed film. Nothing like chase scenes, narrow escapes and things exploding (better this just happens in the movies).

I was surprised that a Canadian movie, *Away From Her*, achieved acclaim in 2007, because it dealt with a different topic, an older man struggling with a wife who suffered from Alzheimer's. That was less Kenny's preference in movie watching, too serious and too sad. Who knows what Kenny's future would have been had he lived his whole life through? Who knows what the fate or destiny is for each one of us? Who knows if an early death "spared" Kenny an eventual tragedy years down the road? Who knows?

What that Canadian flick about Alzheimer's says though, is that the couple did share valuable years together, and that, in itself, is to be cherished "for better or worse." And that's the gift of time that Kenny missed...and being father to his two little kids as they grew up.

On the world stage, movies were made, governments were scheming and currency was going up and down. Meantime, our family pulled in its horns and focused on that couch downstairs in the living room where Kenny lay enduring his cancer day after day.

That microcosm was "our macrocosm", our whole universe, at that time in 2007. We paid no heed to the power struggles of the world, though looking back at it now, nothing new was happening under the sun anyway, outside of Kenny's doors. The whole world didn't matter.

December 2007, *The Bucket List*, came out in theaters. A corporate billionaire and a working class mechanic are at a crossroads in their lives. They share a hospital room and discover they have something in common: a desire to spend the time they have left doing everything they ever wanted to do before they "kick the bucket." They become friends and go on a road trip together, where they learn to live life to the fullest.

Kenny was too weak in December 2007 to go anywhere, weighing all of 100 pounds or less. He would have loved the movie though. I'm sure Kenny would have lived life fuller had he lived. These lines were quoted in Kenny's Wellness Blog from the Tim McGraw song, "Live Like You Were Dying."

> *He said I was in my early forties*
> *with a lot of life before me*
> *when a moment came that stopped me on a dime*
> *and I spent most of the next days*
> *looking at the x-rays*
> *Talking bout the options*
> *and talking bout sweet time*
> *I asked him when it sank in*
> *that this might really be the real end*
> *how's it hit you when you get that kinda news*
> *man what'd you do*

He said I was finally the husband
that most the time I wasn't
and I became a friend a friend would like to have
and all the sudden going fishin
wasn't such an imposition
and I went three times that year I lost my dad
well I finally read the good book
and I took a good long hard look
at what I'd do if I could do it all again
        (#1country song 2004)

But time took everything away from Kenny and did not give him a second chance to be the husband he could have been, to go fishing with his own dad and his little kids or to read *The Good Book* in depth (and more often, though he did read it in his last months).

It's time to bring in the laundry. It gets dark by 5:00 p.m. and I need to put together the ingredients for waffles while "The whole world's cagey...crazy." I just love FM 96.3's slogan, which is what the world needs now (besides love, sweet love): "Beautiful music for a crazy world."

CHAPTER 32

Anwar Knight
Shouts From His Soapbox

Anwar's Fight with Cancer
Tuesday, November 20, 2010

Most Ontarians have heard of Anwar Knight's battle with cancer over the past year in 2010. He's the anchor on the CTV-Toronto news station. He wrote a Blog too about his cancer (courtesy of the CTV web site) and so had a great platform in which to express his thoughts, entitled: "Anwar's Journey – The hodgepodge of an optimist."

Maybe this makes anything that Kenny wrote moot because it was said again by someone who was better known than Kenny.

Kenny had his face in front of a computer screen most of the time, working quietly and privately out of his home in his basement, designing beautiful web sites for which he even won an award in Niagara. His face was not on provincial television, prognosticating weather for Ontario viewers.

That being said, the two men had a story to tell, similar in many ways. No matter how futile they felt the effort might have been, writing about a personal battle with cancer was therapeutic, and it had to be done from an internal need to share your feelings about an affliction.

Both Kenny and Anwar asked "Why Me?" and both wanted to have their story told and their anguish shared. Kenny wrote so much in his Blog that was so much like Anwar's comments. Sadly all of Kenny's written sentiments disappeared when he was too sick to pay his server the renewal fee for his Blog.

Anwar's words are preserved and are so much reminiscent of what Kenny originally wrote and felt, that I feel I am indeed fortunate to have discovered Anwar's online treasure trove:

Anwar's Journey

**The Hodgepodge
Of An Optimist**

Why me? Why not me ?

Anwar Knight
Published Wednesday, May 12, 2010 2:53PM EDT

So just where does one begin when it comes to a life-changing journey like this? What do I have to say, and perhaps more realistically, who really wants to hear about it?

I guess, if nothing else, there may be one person -- just one, who may be dealing with a similar challenge in life. Maybe he or she will find comfort in knowing indeed they are not alone. Stuff like this happens every second, of every day. Yes, of course, you think 'Why Me'? I say -- it may be more appropriate to think 'Why not me'?

When diagnosed with cancer, any cancer, you are forever inducted into a club. Like it or not, (and who are we kidding -- no one likes it) there is a stigma with cancer. A dark cloud that only outsiders, looking in, see. As I sit on my soapbox here, let me tell you, it's not always doom and gloom.
  (Anwar Knight: 12. May 2010 14:53)

*****

Kenny tried to be optimistic through his 10 month struggle. He cut a CD of his songs and held a fundraiser at the Beamsville High-School in June of 2007 where T-shirts were sold advertising the slogan: *"I Blog for Hope...I Blog with Ken!"*

He remarked, that summer, that he was amazed how local newspapers picked up his story and about how gratified he was that he could share his story with others. He didn't know how the news had spread. Maybe it wasn't just me, but I took hours to contact all the newspapers I could find, from Hamilton to Niagara Falls that summer, to let the media know about Kenny's fight and about his Blog. So Kenny did have a public relations agent!

But right now, I feel like I'm "runnin' against the wind" with this story because "who really wants to hear about negative stuff anyway?"

Anwar did a fantastic job on his soapbox in his Blog. It's a more recent story with more public exposure than what Kenny ever managed from his little office in his basement. Kenny's Blog is now lost and Anwar's story, thank goodness, was preserved through a high profile job.

So what's the sense of doing a retell from two lousy posts and some snippets that I lifted from Kenny's Blog before it disappeared? What can you say from a smattering of things!

I've gotten a string of rejection letters to date from publishers about retelling Kenny's struggle with cancer, and that certainly has taken the wind out of my sails to continue writing. Maybe if I step away for a while and take some time off?

I don't even know why I'm doing this except to keep me busy over the winter months with the hopes, I guess, that I leave something of Kenny and myself behind, in case my leukemia kicks up again. My count has climbed slowly but steadily from 12 in 2003 to 14 in 2010. Not a good sign.

I have a reprieve apparently until it hits 20 and that's when treatment kicks in for me at the Juravinski Clinic. I don't want to deal with the oncologists locally despite the new hospital being built in St. Catharines with a target date of 2013 for completion. Why don't I want to be treated locally? I don't trust them. Just a personal feeling; I'd rather go to a bigger city.

_____

It's been cold and raining all morning. I don't know, maybe it's the weather outside that's making me feel low. I discovered Anwar's Blog just this morning and I feel like what I'm doing is just plain redundant. I feel like my writing here is a useless exercise, telling a story about cancer that nobody wants to hear...and then those rejection letters from publishers!

155

I don't have much to work with and I feel pretty small, pounding out my thoughts on Kenny and myself from this soapbox in my little study on this old computer (2002) that Kenny, by the way, built for me.

Kenny was still optimistic from March to October but in November 2007 he had lost so much weight! He looked like a yardstick and was really weak.

He got frustrated one evening and told the family gathered around the kitchen table: "You don't understand! You're not me!" He practically shouted it out with a hoarse voice that was constricted by cancer.

What could we say or do? Pray? Prayer didn't help, we prayed right to the end in January but there was no answer, at least not the answer we wanted. In that respect, Kenny had a different journey than Anwar.

Anwar says: "Whatever you were doing is put on hold and you have a new mission in life -- to get better." Kenny put his web design business on hold, closed up shop and from his couch in the basement concentrated on healing. When would healing come? It never came. Whenever anyone visited, little Braeden always told them, "Daddy, sleeping."

Kenny read *The Secret* by Rhonda Byrne, calling upon the Universe to cure him through the law of attraction with positive thoughts.

That book on positive thinking was the rave back then, in 2007. He bought into the idea that you are meant to have an amazing life, you can make your own destiny by just willing it.

Well, he didn't get better. He got worse and died on January 18, 2008.

As to Rhonda Byrne's book, I think it made her millions; it was a good sell. She says that Jesus was privy to "the secret", shared by other greats like Plato, Newton, Edison, Beethoven, Einstein and Churchill!

Now if Jesus was privy to the law of attraction of the universe, why was he crucified?

It's also hard to swallow why 6 million Jews were incinerated in concentration camps during WW II -- because they had negative thoughts?

According to her claim, the universe only gives people what they ask for! That claim sounds so delicious, so wise, so insightful! It's ludicrous!

It's kind of obvious (duh) that the power of positive thinking helps to attract lots of friends and helps you get ahead. That idea isn't new and it sure isn't a secret!

But sometimes things just happen outside of someone's control and then you cope the best you can with whatever talent, courage and heart you have. Sometimes despite everything, you just bite the dust and die!

Kenny faced the inevitable, I think, by December of 2007. All the prayer, all the hope, he and we put into his cure seemed to be for nothing. As he got thinner, weaker and so drawn out, he could hardly stand up near the end. We held on to faith in the face of futility. We had nothing else. What does a person cling to when there's nothing left? Hope and faith in something because it's a need.

CHAPTER 33

Anwar's Subtype

Anwar informs people: "Thankfully, and I really mean that, I have been diagnosed with a subtype of Hodgkin's Lymphoma that is thought of as a research success story."

Apparently, Kenny also might have had Hodgkin's Lymphoma but he also had Epstein-Barr Syndrome which complicated any treatment, plus he wanted to have a *Voice for Choice* with alternative natural medicine. So, the stories are similar and yet not the same, and the outcomes were so tragically different in our family.

Anwar respected his doctors at the big hospital, Princess Margaret in Toronto, and was grateful to specialists in the system there who would take care of him: "Extremely gifted people, along with lots of dollars, have figured out how to treat and cure this disease. But it's far from the only one."

Kenny experienced nothing but frustration locally in St. Catharines and had no respect for "these clowns." He felt he was misdiagnosed and felt his immune system was threatened more by chemo and radiation, because of his Epstein-Barr Syndrome, than by a choice for natural herbs and medicines.

Anwar Knight was treated in Toronto and Kenny did not hear from the Princess Margaret Hospital until it was too late and then (I think) was rejected because of territorial rights with local doctors. Anwar was cured and Kenny died.

*****

Snippets from Kenny's Blog expose conflicting reports, stating he's stage 4, and then another report says he's stage 3, and then another report it's back to stage 4 again.

I'm What??!! AGAIN??!!
24. May 2007 @ 11:53

[family doctor receives fax from Princess Margaret, Dr. M shows it to Kenny]
"upon further review of his files, we think Mr. Janzen actually may be in stage 3 of his cancer and therefore elegible for radiation, surgery and other curative approaches...."

We just heard this garbage last Monday (the 14th) from these clowns. And then they kyboshed the whole thing by phone the next day telling me that OOPS! upon even FURTHER review I indeed was stage 4. So NOW - a week and a half later... my doctor gets a report dated May the 23rd that says I'm stage 3 and that my case will be presented to the "tumor board' at the hospital on May 25th.

After about 5 min – Sue who is a nurse was able to get one of the interns familliar with my case on the phone who confirmed that yes - the report was just typed wrong. OOPS!!!! Their official diagnosis for me was still stage four lung cancer NOT stage three. I should sue these idiots for gross neglegence and for causing mental anguish.

It was the infectious disease doctors' rock solid opinion that in NO way could my chronic Epstein-Barr cause my Lymph nodes to swell. <-- REMEMBER THIS!

3 minutes research on google search: yes Epstein-Barr syndrome can cause enlarged lymph nodes! ...

Till then!
The Medical Mystery that is Me :) | Comments (10)

Snippet: Kenny is really ticked off at the delays and mixed reports he is getting...

Is that a pogo stick? No it's just Ken!
26. May 2007 @ 09:34

Third message
..."Hi this is Dr. [medical oncologist] (name removed) calling from Princess Margaret Hospital in Toronto. I'm just calling to see if you have arranged for any treatments locally. *We wouldn't want you to fall through the cracks now would we...*

My buddy Jim and I were joking on the phone yesterday afternoon comically imitating the doctors saying;
"Oh...So sorry Ken...you're gonna die now."
"Oh No...our mistake Ken! You're not dead yet - here's some hope."
"OOPS!! Did we give you hope yesterday? Sorry about that - we need that back"
"WAIT!! Here Ken!! Here's some more hope we found on the floor in the corner"
"Our Bad! That wasn't hope - that was just a dust bunny...sorry. Just go home and die."

Like I said - at least I can laugh about it...

One of these days I'm gonna take my story public! To let other cancer sufferers out there know that they are being blindsided and 'herded" like cattle into a system whose only intent is to kill them slowly while making as MUCH money off them as they can in the process. Sound a little callous? Believe me - that IS what's going on! Big Pharmaceutical companies run the medical show folks. It's that simple.

Till tomorrow!
The Medical Mystery that is Me :) | Comments (4)

*****

Life Gives Us Only What We Can Handle?

I think it was in Anwar's Blog, but it doesn't matter, where a well-wisher wrote: "Life gives us only what we can handle." That is simply not true! Sometimes life gives us more than we can handle, and the fact is, we don't have a choice in the matter.

Kenny started out with hope, then came to acceptance and finally death. It helped to have family and friends see him through his journey to the end. Kenny didn't want to go to the hospital; he died at home.

I'm sure that if Kenny would have survived, he would have had a new appreciation for life. Anwar Knight does and I do too! Especially after seeing my brother-in-law decline, go into a coma and then actually die. It hurt. The whole family was gathered around the hospital bed that had been carted down into the basement of his house. He wanted to die at home. We heard his last breath.

Anwar ends his posts with this comment (so Kenny-like): "There are never ever any guarantees in life ... from here on, I will make each day count ... let the journey begin..."

He adds a little quote from a famous man:
Attitude is a little thing that makes a big difference.
~Winston Churchill

There are a total of 266 comments from well wishers to Anwar's post in this Blog. Kenny's usual numbers were 25, 35, maybe 45 comments at the most, except when some porno program threw links into the comment boxes, booting the numbers above 400 one day and 500 another day. The number even blasted to over 3,000 during the summer, where Kenny, I think, cleaned house. It was difficult to clean out this garbage from the Blog and the family wondered who would do such a thing where a person had cancer?

Even that part of the story needs telling, to yell out that some things need to be sacred and left alone by hackers!

Kenny would have been glad to see Anwar on his soapbox writing his thoughts down in public because people often get courage from each other, sharing their problems with others. Kenny would also have loved Anwar's choice titles:

Weather Weenie: Anwar says Hello, Making Lemonade, Love and Laughter, Why Me? Why Not Me?

Kenny had a similar knack for words.   Thanks Anwar, for sharing.
I hope that someday this little bit of Kenny that I'm writing about
gets out into the public...and with it, a little of me.

CHAPTER 34

Time for a Tea-Break:

I've invited Lynne and Michael Kositsky over for tea and chocolate cake at 3 p.m. They are the Jewish couple who bought a house down the street last year, ironically right opposite the United Mennonite Church. I teased them that I'd promise not to convert them.

Lynne is a published author of children's stories usually with a Jewish theme. She's also written some things about adult historical fiction. Michael is a composer. They must have liked the small town atmosphere in Vineland after a life in Toronto.

Lynne stood outside my kitchen door shivering and extending a Hanukkah gift to me, a plate wrapped in cellophane replete with Clementines, two doughnuts and Hanukkah "gelt" (i.e. chocolate loonies and toonies).

I plugged in our Christmas lights which made the Great Room look cheery. Lynne talked about her latest collaboration in a book on Oxfordian Shakespeare. I talked about how my so called Blog was turning into a social commentary and possibly a book. Michael invited me over for *Star Trek, The Next Generation* but I declined wanting to write more and then having to get supper ready.

After Lynne and Michael left, I lay down for 30 minutes. My battery runs down in waves now-a-days. I listened to the radio 96.3 Classical FM, "Beautiful Music for a Crazy World."

First, Ralph Vaughan Williams' "Fantasia on Green sleeves" and then Dvorak's "Humoresque" played by the cellist Yo Yo Ma and violinist, Itzhak Perlman. How could beautiful music like that come from a human race that kills each other in wars?

My plan for supper was to wrap salmon in aluminum foil and barbecue it. I was making home fries in the frying pan after having cut up Yukon Gold potatoes.

My wife finally came home exhausted after a day with her grade 6 and 7s. We watched *Dragnet* on Retro TV while we ate from our TV trays. The episode was about a woman who had dumped her baby in a garbage can. Dum, da, rum, da...dummmm!

Marjorie is at the church at singing practice for Sunday's worship service this Wednesday evening. Her sinuses usually sabotage her full effort but she needs something to look forward to.

While she's gone, I've taken the opportunity to write about the end of our day and to email Lynne and Michael to thank them for the Hanukkah gift. I quipped that it was my wife who took all of my "gelt" [chocolate money] and left me penniless with only the doughnuts to live on.

I've taken a Tylenol because of a weather headache again; it's bitterly cold outside this evening.

Hanukkah will start tomorrow, Thursday, December 2, 2010. Lynne and Michael invited us to light a Menorah candle last year at their house and that was nice. My headache persists. I'm taping "Human Target" on TV (on our old VCR). Soon by August 2011, our ability to tape anything will disappear with analogue stations going off the air.

I need another lie-down to assuage my headache by listening to beautiful music for a crazy world. Such a true slogan! Do you remember the George Burns and Gracie Allen show? Say Goodnight Gracie!

_____

Thursday, December 2, 2010

Today is a lost day. My migraine is worse. Took another Tylenol. I can hardly think.

I've slept away a good part of the morning and now that I'm up briefly, my eyes are squinty and it hurts like hell to look at anything. I can see where seniors might not want to get up some days.

The sun is breaking through patches of white and blue. We have rainbow dots dancing around in our Great Room, rainbow pixies that fly around the room, spread there by the Austrian crystals hanging at the top of the window. Those rainbow pixies are happier than I am.

Thank goodness music was gentle this morning on FM 96.3 classical radio.

I listened to Andrew Lloyd Weber's *Pie Jesu* sung by Anna Netrebko. It soothed my headache and fit my dolorous mood.

I need to visit old Harry Rittenhouse (102) and Uncle Walter (88) in the United Mennonite Home next week. They might be feeling low too. Today is a lost day.

CHAPTER 35

Picking Up the Kids
Sunday, December 5, 2010

My wife and I picked Braeden and Darriane up this morning at 9 a.m. to take them to Sunday school at the United Mennonite Church. Darriane is going to play Mary in the kids' Christmas program.

We won't be there because we're flying to Fort Lauderdale on the 24th for a one week cruise in the Eastern Caribbean. Maybe Sue and Adam can see Darriane in the play; they would love seeing the kids do their thing. Braeden doesn't pull any punches about when he's bored. He had his transformer and a colouring book to keep busy during Pastor Ross' sermon on Sunday but these things only go so far with a little boy's attention span. He fidgeted with his toys: "When is this done?" he asked plain, straight out. Sigh, give him a few more goldfish crackers to munch!

Lunch at our place means pizza buns, pickles and juice. I must remember not to put the bowl of bread and butter pickles out before the pizza buns are ready. Braeden had almost all the pickles gobbled up by the time we sat down to eat. He loves to pray though, and will rattle off a blessing for anything under the sun. He goes on and on (with eyes closed)! I think he likes the attention. I try to show an example in brevity when it's my turn: "Thank you God for this food. Amen."

After lunch, I interviewed a couple for a wedding next August in Niagara-on-the-Lake and got the job. Then the kids decorated the lower half of the Christmas tree while Marjorie decorated the higher part.

We unpacked Santa's village which always gets put on the Christmas skirt at the bottom of the tree. Braeden grabbed too many of the porcelain houses and dropped one on top of the other with a crash. The library splintered into many pieces which required careful picking up and vacuuming. Braeden ran off crying and my wife talked to him in a soothing voice about handling Santa's village, one piece at a time.

She told both kids that this village was special and one that their daddy had actually hand-painted. She showed them the Ken Janzen signature at the bottom of the broken piece and the year: '97.

We inherited the village after Kenny died and maybe someday one or both of the kids will get those pieces back for keepsakes. Well, Braeden's crying was short-lived and pretty soon he was back to grabbing up other buildings for the village with my wife having to tell him all over again: "Be careful!. One at a time, Braeden! One at a time!"

The Sunday visit is never complete without stopping at my sister-in-law's, Marilyn, to see the little shitsu doggie, Bria. The game is never ending with the kids throwing a little red ball down the hallway and the little mutt chasing the ball and playing keep-aways with it, while the kids chase her down. Then we make the final drop and deliver "the package", i.e. the kids, at their mom Sue's place, and make our escape home to recover. I guess that's the advantage of being uncle and aunt (or grandparents).

We picked Braeden and Darriane up again after supper, this Sunday evening, and took them to the live Christmas show at Calvary Church in Beamsville. The church creates these staged acting scenes in different spots all around the church, with volunteer actors dressed in costume and live animals (donkeys, goats and miniature horses – no camels though) to recount the life and times at the birth of Christ.

It was CCccoold out there, so we were bundled up. Different stations had actual campfires going in the parking lot to give the sense of being there in olden times. There's hot chocolate and cookies afterwards. We've taken the kids to this re-enactment for several years now and they like the acting and the animals.

Braeden is getting to be a handful about having his way though, in this and that, and needs holding onto in the parking lot because he'll just run off by himself.

My wife and I are glad to have the kids over as uncle and aunt but we are most happy to send them back home to mom's when we're tuckered out. You have to be young to have and handle kids! Marjorie and I have been spared that responsibility or blessing. Depends how you look at it.

I teased my wife on Monday morning, while she got ready for work: "Imagine having to get the kids ready too?"

"I can hardly do me!" she groaned. "I'm already 10 minutes behind."

I helped with breakfast by chopping almonds and doing the 6 minutes for her oatmeal in the microwave, while she walked on the treadmill. We're not perky at that hour anymore, maybe never were. It is incredible to listen to Mike Duncan and Jean Stillwell first thing in the morning on FM 96.3. I don't know if it's their nature or their paycheque that puts such zeal and zest into their voices first thing in the morning?

Oh well, we are an older couple. after all. Nothing beats youth and health! I think youth is wasted on the young! You have to have a sense of humour in all this. I've often said to Harry Rittenhouse, my 103 year old step grandfather-in-law, "Harry, at least we still got our good looks!"

I've got a toothache today! It's time to phone the dentist. I hate root canals. They remind me of writing a book. Well, maybe not completely, just in spots. There are moments when I'm in my element when I write something with flare and with deep insight. Then, I really feel happy. Other times, I have the urge to push the delete button. So easy to do now-a-days. At least, with burning a manuscript, you could still retrieve some pages from the fire. Maybe that's all the Yin and Yang of things.

Damn this tooth. It's such a pain! Dentists sure make a lot of money. I hope my dentist is worth his paycheque!

CHAPTER 36

Listening to the Radio
Tuesday, December 7, 2010

Our new alarm clock is our radio, automatically tuned to Classical FM 96.3 at 5:45 a.m. Better to wake up to music, than to the old buzzer we used to have that felt like a Skilsaw cutting through a 2x4. It was annoying! Well, it's time to roll out of bed. This was the announcement I just heard on the radio:

Canadian Journalist Mark Dailey Dies at 57
Mark Dailey, an American-born TV journalist for Canadian station CityTV, has died of cancer at the age of 57. This was Dailey's second bout with cancer.

How sad.

My wife and I are sensitively tuned to the word "cancer" now-a-days. We hate the word.

But it's time to get up. I prop myself up, my left hand braced against the edge of the bed, taking a breather before I actually stand up and get my wife's terrible tasting concoction ready of 25 lemon drops in a glass. She mixes that with Aloe Vera juice which is supposed to kill pathogens in the body. So far, no difference to her health!

My Brother-in-Law
Got Sick

I waddle back to bed for another 10 minutes and listen to the *Harp Concerto* by Karl Ditters von Dittersdorf. Restful piece of music, but where did he get that name?

It's very nippy outside.   My wife doesn't want me to go to Kitchener today to visit my mom and sister in the Trinity Seniors' Home. Blowing wind and snow.

I have chores to do instead: hand laundry, another pile of bras (is there no end?) and cut up another pomegranate and mango. Well, who am I to complain?   With two nervous breakdowns, leukemia, an artificial aortic valve and a body that's 64, I feel like a retread. If I were not married to my wife, I could very well be a street person somewhere, and obviously this book would never see the light of day.

What would I do if I were single and homeless? Actually, I'd probably move to a small town somewhere in Newfoundland and become a newspaper reporter there all over again. It's what I know best. But that would replay a big struggle in my past.

I didn't like waking up to that radio announcement this morning. Dailey had announced in the fall that he was suffering from kidney cancer. That ultimately spread to his lungs. How come we hear so much of these things now-a-days?

My head feels just a cotton ball today. Fluffy and achy. The word "lassitude" comes to mind. Certainly not "chipper or perky". Lou Asner said something like, "I hate perky" to Mary Tyler Moore in the old sit-com.

I saw my family doctor today because my migraine was just killing me all of yesterday. He gave me two free samples of *Axert*. I took one before supper and one before bedtime. I had a little dizzy spell after supper and lay down for a bit until the *Big Bang Theory* came on TV.

"Wake me for my favourite show," I said to my wife. "I want to see what stupid things Sheldon does today."

I read the little booklet that came with *Axert* on side effects. Actually I found this amusing: sleepiness, dizziness and guess what? – headache! Here is a headache medication that can cause headaches! How can that be?

Is there a mad scientist in the pharmacy lab somewhere mixing fuming potions together, casting a spell as he does so with a gleam in his eye, "Abracadabra, let this headache potion create more headaches! That will be $5.00 a pill!"

I just saw a commercial during my other favourite show, *Peter Gunn*, over the noon hour on *Avandia*. It's supposed to be a drug for diabetes but lawyers are advertising possible law suits against the company because the drug is linked to heart attacks and death and so families may be entitled to legal compensation they deserve.

Now-a-days, there's all kinds of disclaimers with new drugs that come out on the market and one wonders, how can these things ever get passed by the Food and Drug Association or Health Canada?

Sometimes the side effects are worse than the things they are supposed to cure! Anyway, it's nippy outside and as I said, my body feels like it's in a state of "lassitude". My tooth is only slightly aching now. (could it be that *Axert* is exerting a magical pharmacy property on me?)

Unusual Types
Thursday, December 9, 2010

What I like about *Peter Gunn* is that it finds roles for unusual types of people, like the dwarf, Babby, under 4', who sells information to Gunn for a price.

In yesterday's episode, entitled "Blind Item", Babby has gotten himself a membership to an exclusive golf and country club and so he's practicing his swing indoors. Babby, under 4', coaches Gunn on his swing and this is quite amusing.

Babby was played by Billy Barty, a very recognizable face from many films.

In the real world, Billy Barty was a crusader for the social acceptance of dwarfs and the founder of *The Little People of America Inc.*, a fact which underscored the unusual talents which characterized the old black and white *Peter Gunn* shows from the late 1950s to early 60s. Barty hated the term "dwarf". He was militant about people of his size being called, "little people".

Lloyd Lindroth was another unusual talent who played Keith Tucker, the wrongly accused musician in this *Blind Item* episode.

There is a great scene where Lieutenant Jacoby comes into the nightclub to arrest Tucker for suspicion of murder but before the cops arrest him, they let the suspect finish his harp playing and the camera alternates shots between him actually playing the harp and seeing his silhouette perform with nimble finger-work against the backlight of a moon.

The old *Peter Gunn* series has cameos like this regularly featuring people with unusual talents. Lloyd Lindroth is actually the musical genius playing the harp during this crime show!

Lindroth had the reputation in the 1960s of being "the Liberace of the Harp" and this just illustrates the artistic excellence that the old detective series had in bringing in such cameo performances.

I loved Lindroth's hairdo, which was called a "ducktail" in my day in the early sixties, a style very popular and worn by one of my grade 8 classmates, Jim Moyer, back in 1962.

Anyway, the TV audience finds out that "the writer" is the real killer at the end. He gets shot by Gunn in a chase. Forest Graham is the writer, a gossip columnist in this case, so he's a hack and (I suppose) deserves to die.

There is one scene that is done very well. The character, Forest Graham, sits at his typewriter in a smoking jacket. There is lovely classical music filling his apartment to inspire his writing. [Tongue in cheek: some Muse for a gossip column!]

Graham types the last sentence with a flourish, gets up and pours himself a well-deserved brandy.

His apartment is resplendent with Greek statuary and large paintings, everything an author should enjoy within a cultured ambiance. But a gossip column? Really?

I chuckled at Graham's smoking jacket and his plush ambiance for establishing a writer's mood because right now I'm wearing a tattered sweatshirt, jeans and longjohns, because I just got back from a snowy drive to the dentist's, and I'm caressing a cup of instant coffee to warm up before I get into my mood for writing.

There is so much talent that has gone under the bridge in these old movies, washed away with the waves of time. Entertainment that people don't watch anymore. How sad. My nostalgic 1950s are gone! Like the hockey game, I need a replay! I miss it so much!

CHAPTER 37

_____

The World As a Fruitcake
Friday, December 10, 2010

In today's _Peter Gunn_ episode "Come Dance With Me and Die" (1961), the story dealt with a gangster who terrorized a young woman over what she heard as a dental nurse working inside a prison.

She gets mugged in an alley but is rescued when a cab driver breaks things up. The cab driver calls Peter Gunn to investigate the mugging: "The whole world is a fruitcake!" says the cab driver.

The nurse, Ruthy, has been working as a dancehall girl in a nightclub trying to hide from the world. [Don't ask me. I don't write these things!]

Male customers buy tickets to dance with the girls. Her friend, Candy, tries to protect Ruthy when a crooked PI comes snooping around but isn't successful in finding out Ruthy's whereabouts. Peter Gunn comes into the nightclub too, buys a ticket and tries to get Ruthy's address from Candy so he can track her down.

He's not successful either in finding out the girl's hideout. He leaves and on the street is almost blasted away in a drive-by shooting. Gunn ducks into a corridor and wins Candy's trust. At the end, there's a huge shoot-out between the cops and the gangsters in Doyle's Nightclub. Not just a shoot-out but a hand to hand combat between cops and robbers. The cops win.

Does any of this make sense? I didn't think so, but it was fun watching it.

There are three conclusions I gleaned from this episode:
1. the whole world is nutty as a fruitcake!
2. drive-by shootings are cowardly and remind me of the road-side bombings in Afghanistan.
3. at least hand to hand combat was still practiced years ago, in old black and white movies, whereas modern terrorism has sanitized killings with roadside bombings...safety for the killers and a practice of cowards!
4. old black and white action movies don't necessarily make sense but they are fun to watch.

CHAPTER 38

A Little Mennonite History
Friday, December 17, 2010

5:45 a.m. We woke to *Silent Night* sung by the Priests on Classical 96.3 FM. "At least, it's not oompa music," I said, swinging my feet out of bed.

I drove my wife to school and then bided [bade, baded, bidded?] my time at *Tim Horton's*, reading Uncle Walter's book on the Mennonites. I recognized Uncle Siegfried Janzen and Anni and Hans Geddert in the old photographs.

Uncle Siegfried worked hard for *Mennonite Central Committee* to get many Mennonites over to Canada before and after World War II. I couldn't help but find it ironic to be sitting at *Tim Horton's*, luxuriating with my medium French Vanilla, paging through a book on Mennonites escaping the persecution in Russia. My own family escaped the barracks in Austria, and got into Canada in 1954 through Pier 21 in Halifax.

Road to Freedom (publ. 2000) painted a great historical panorama of Mennonites in Russia from 1917 into the post-war years of WW II, using personal anecdotes and old pictures of those times.

Communist Russia blamed Mennonite colonies in the Ukraine for not learning the Russian language. The secret police sent "the black raven" (the paddy wagon) to homes to round up the men, take them to prison and they disappeared never to be heard from again by their families.

When the Nazi army rolled Eastwards, many Mennonites actually thought they were being rescued from the Communists, not knowing what was happening to the Jews. They were considered German citizens in foreign lands and promised a better life outside of Russia. The Nazis expelled Poles from north-western Poland to make room for Mennonite refugees who were considered Volksdeutsche (extended German speaking peoples).

Some Mennonites found this new life difficult to accept, first of all, because Polish people had to be dispossessed of their homes (which they could identify with). Secondly, the "real Germans" from The Reich took the best farms and estates in the formerly Polish regions and they showed contempt for second class Germans, those labelled the "Volksdeutsche" from Ukraine and the "Scwarzmeerdeutsche", that is, Black Sea Germans, who couldn't speak proper high-German.

In terms of discrimination, the Mennonites felt that they were still under Communism, only under a different name. They hadn't yet come to a true home of freedom (p. 33).

I found excerpts from Irene Jantz's diary touching, recalling her move East, as part of the Nazi evacuation to escape the Red Army. She mentions Linz, Austria.

I was born in Asten, which is just 30 minutes outside of Linz. Just another 30 minutes in another direction was Mauthausen, the concentration camp where thousands of Jews, Poles, Russians and Slavs ended their lives in gas chambers. I was born in 1946. Irene Jantz was born in 1925 and so she had vivid memories of life as a refugee, being separated from mother and father. She recalls being registered as a German citizen in Linz and then sleeping in soft beds in the barracks.

I remember living in barracks until 1954, sleeping on hay mattresses. When I was an 8 year old boy, my family moved to Canada. I had rheumatic fever and tuberculosis in Austria, with 2 years spent in a sanatorium. I loved those portions of Irene Jantz's diary where she looked up at the moon and the stars for hope late at night:

> March 18. How small one appears as one gazes at the stars in the heavens! As a worm crawling in the dust of the earth, a continuous coming and going completing the eternal cycle of life and death. In the stars, however, one senses the highest, yet unreachable longing of man, who is always striving to reach eternal freedom. (p. 49)

Irene Jantz married Jake Isaac and they lived in Edmonton, Alberta. In my mind, her diary compared well in literary stature to Anne Frank, *The Diary of A Young Girl*. Of course, one precious young lady perished in Bergen Belsen and the other went on to make a life in Canada. I can't help but think of another comparison here to Kenny and Anwar Knight, even if it's a thread of a comparison, one dying from cancer and the other being freed from it. Irene (Jantz) Isaac died of cancer herself in 1996 at the age of 71, but at least, one can say, she had a life.

I closed the book at Timmy's and made my grocery run first to Sobey's, Rexall Pharmacy and then to No Frills for an Oh, Henry chocolate bar.

I coasted back to Timmy's for a regular coffee, another French Vanilla and a chunky chocolate chip cookie and then made a beeline for home, stuffing my frozen veggies and Eggo Waffles in the freezer. And then another beeline to the UM Home to visit 102 year-old Harry Rittenhouse and 88 year-old Uncle Walter. I was armed with coffees, a large cookie and that Oh Henry chocolate bar.

*****

Harry snoozed in his easy chair. His ghetto blaster was playing Christmas music. I shut it off. Stood over him with the coffee and cookie until he woke.

"Watcha been doing Harry?"
"Nothin' much, if I can help it."

He thanked me for the cookie and started nibbling. He figured this one was just as hard as the other one I brought him the other day.

"You can sharpen your teeth on them," he said chuckling. Harry was congested this morning and coughing a bit more than usual. I could hear a tiny wheeze when he breathed.

I told him about the Mennonite book I was reading. He's never been in a war.

"I was too young for the first one and then when I got old enough, I was too old for the second one."

He figured war was the business of politicians and big money and he had no use for any of it. I mentioned Hitler and Stalin and he said that they were just men who got a stubborn idea in their head and then just made trouble for everybody else.

"But what're ya gonna do?" he said. He munched on his cookie.

All his working life, Harry had worked for *Vineland Growers* and had 40 workers under him. He was proud of that. When fruit growing and picking was out of season, he'd go hunting and fishing and trek all over hill and dale, with his favourite dog, Bing.

Maybe all that trekking and physical work gave Harry the gift of longevity, plus whatever he had in his DNA to begin with. Harry doesn't read, doesn't like it, though he can see quite well through his glasses. "Never had no interest," he told me. And yet, his mind is as sharp as a tack and he comes across with words that are pithy like little jewels. I asked him if I should turn the Christmas music back on when I leave. "Suit yourself," he said. "I listen to it all day. You get so's you're sick of it." I'd put a straw in his coffee cup earlier. He always lets the cup sit because he doesn't like it hot. He took a slurp. "Ah," he sighed with appreciation. I asked him if Bob Burtch had been in earlier this week to see him. He didn't recollect.

"Couldn't tell ya. My memory's gone once you leave."

I got up to go. He thanked me again and called me Bob. And then corrected himself, shaking his head, "I mean..." I interrupted, "That's okay Harry. You can call me John..." He laughed and said, "Okay John. See ya. Stay out of trouble."

Uncle Walter was most happy to see me pull out the *Oh, Henry* chocolate bar from my coat pocket. He said he knew just what to do with it. I told him I really enjoyed the stories in the Mennonite book I borrowed from him. His brother, Siegfried Janzen, was in one of the pictures. I said I wanted to borrow his history book for another week. "As long as you want," he agreed.

I mentioned it was almost time for lunch. Uncle Walter observed that there were only 3 men in the dining room and all the rest were women. I teased him about having a good choice of girlfriends. He ignored the comment and told me the story of how he met his wife, Annie. Aunt Annie died of cancer some years back.

In 1950, a meeting of new Mennonite Canadians was organized by churches at Niagara-on-the-Lake.

"They came from as far away as Leamington," recalled Uncle Walter. He was late and had trouble finding a parking spot. He sat at the back of the church and enjoyed the singing program put on by various churches. Four groups of girls' quartets sang. Aunt Annie was a young girl in the quartet from Leamington and Uncle Walter spotted her right away. He couldn't keep his eyes off her.

"That's the girl I'm going to marry," he thought to himself. He knew the pastor at the Mennonite Church in Leamington, so he thought he'd ask for her phone number through him. Unknown to Uncle Walter, Aunt Annie was helping that very pastor out because the wife had health problems. The pastor gave him their number.

When Uncle Walter phoned, Aunt Annie answered. He said to her over the phone, "I've never met you but I'm looking for a wife." Aunt Annie's response was quick and simple: "Sure, I'll be your wife." And that was that! Uncle Walter chuckled over that memory.

I told him about how I met Marjorie in Grande Prairie, Alberta. I'd buy supper tickets at the Hillcrest Centre (where she taught all day). She needed to take walks to get out of the building and so she went from table to table asking for a male escort because the

Centre was close to a bad part of town. I'd always volunteer.
There came a day when I told Marjorie that I wanted to court her.
And that was that!

Snow was starting to blow around just outside of Uncle Walter's
window and I said my goodbye. "Make sure the chocolate bar
lasts you all weekend," I told him. His jackknife still lay open on
his table ready for his apples and his chocolate bars.

CHAPTER 39

Shameless Idealists
Tuesday, December 21, 2010

I slipped to the TV at 10:00 a.m. for a quick break and snack (yogurt and strawberries). Craig Kielburger was hosting a special guest, Betty Williams, in a 7 part series on a show called *Shameless Idealists.* Betty was originally described by newspapers as a mere housewife in 1976 when she petitioned for the fighting in Northern Ireland to stop.

She heard shots exchanged between the IRA and British soldiers and witnessed a car careening around the corner which slammed into 3 innocent children and killed them. She became a champion for children and for peace in a split country.

Betty and her friend, Mairead Corrigan-Maguire, were awarded the Nobel Peace Prize for their petitions among mothers for peace. They created an entire movement that changed Ireland.

"Somebody had to do something." "Every child killed, every child that dies of starvation, illness that can be prevented or wars they don't declare, is a mother's labour spurned."

Betty is a Catholic and strong believer in God who knows Archbishop Tutu and His Holiness, the Dalai Lama personally. She sees the role of mothers as a sacred duty. She is outraged that children are caught in the crossfire and killed in adult wars in so many countries. "It says, Thou shalt not kill. It doesn't say, you can kill for this reason or that reason." "How dare anybody destroy that gift, that God gave you to give life."

When people said to her, your actions are futile, her response was "get out of my way." "The biggest killer in our world is apathy or it's none of my business."

She defined herself as a mother, number one but she also commented: "I have never met an ordinary housewife!" She disagreed with what she sees through the media which focuses on what's wrong in the world. "Do a non-violent way of protest about newspapers. Stop buying them!" "Hit them in the pocket book."

I guess the same goes for TV and all the channel packages you can get, hundreds of stations. Stop buying them! Doesn't the time wasted there, take away from real-life? My attitude is the same for social networking on the computer, *Facebook* and *Twitter*. You can really twitter your time and then your life away!

Well, it's almost time for lunch and for *Peter Gunn*. That's different! You have to have some entertainment but you don't have to make a life of it, whether it's movies, TV, newspapers, email or *Facebook*. I guess I won't hit the delete button yet on this wintery project of mine. This writing is the only thing that preoccupies my mind during December, while the snow blows outside and while Marjorie is at work with her grade 6/7 kids.

Maybe writing my thoughts down, whether it's about my own life or about what Kenny went through, is worthwhile after all. I'll keep pecking away at the keyboard, publisher or no publisher, whether it's the sound of a tree falling in the forest with nobody to listen to the sound or not!

I'm glad that there are shameless idealists like Betty Williams. Keep on staying healthy, Betty, and keep on having a voice for children and for peace around the world. There's enough woe in the world that somebody has to say or do something to make the mess better.

Usually I turn commercials on mute. They are louder than the regular programming anyway. This morning I listened to advertising from the *Christian Child Fund Catalog*. I donated $50 to give some family 5 chickens in a poor country. Marjorie and I have also donated to *World Vision* at different times, as well as the *Mennonite Central Committee*.

I just wish third world countries could have honest elections and that they developed infrastructures for their own economic success.

Haiti, for example, after a year since its horrendous earthquake has made little progress in recovery and yet, the land has so much potential. I remember getting Care packages as a kid in Austria in 1950. My family really appreciated gifts of clothes and food after World War II while we lived in barracks. Every little bit helps and every mother, like Betty Williams, makes a difference!

Good Luck to Democracy
Wednesday, December 22, 2010

A referendum is taking place in Southern Sudan from January 9th until January 15th 2011, on whether or not the region should remain a part of Sudan or be independent.

The North is mostly Islam and the south tolerates Christianity. Usually, violence accompanies such a process in these split countries. Good luck to democracy!

I'm thinking of Haiti's chaotic elections held just this month, almost a year after the earthquake. Going further abroad and further back, I'm also thinking of North and South Korea, North and South Ireland, Israel and Palestine and even Cyprus within my memory.

Killings besmirched the history of all of these countries because of a difference of opinion and culture.

I sometimes wonder if Canada has made the right decision in trying to create a cultural Mozaic or is that just a dreamy notion devoid of reality? I still find John Lennon's song, *Imagine*, a nice thought, where everyone can live in peace in all the world. But that could just be imagining.

The pro-South Sudan independence newsletter South Sudan Nation notes: "In reality, all the imperfections that South Sudan has—tribalism, nepotism, cronyism, mismanagement of the national resources, cattle rustling, tribal wars, civil wars, visionary-less leaders to mention but just a few—are all the trademarks of each and every country on the Africa continent..." (Wikipedia)

I'm listening to tidbits of global news from the safety of my home in Canada, while munching my breakfast of waffles and sipping my morning coffee in front of my TV (usually turned to Canada AM).

Marjorie and I are catching a plane on Friday morning from the Buffalo airport to fly to Fort Lauderdale where we embark on a 7 day cruise in the Eastern Caribbean. I'm hoping for pretty aqua-marine water, lots of sun and absolutely no worldly news!

CHAPTER 40

Christmas Cruise 2010
December 24 – December 31

THE CRUISE

I've always hated the security checks at the American border but that's par for the course now-a-days. We showed our passports (which was not a requisite until recently). It used to be: "What's your citizenship?" "Canadian!" "Purpose of the visit?" "A cruise from Fort Lauderdale." "Okay, go ahead!"

At the airport, we had to put our shoes into a plastic container to be scanned (no explosives in my soles!) and then walk through the body scanner. I was born with a guilty face (maybe because I was raised a Catholic) but thank Mary, Mother of God, I was waved through! Marjorie even had to pass her cane through the X-ray machine, in case there were any secret weapons inside. I think Steed in the old *Avengers* series used to hide a stabbing utensil inside his cane.

But since 9/11, I don't blame airports for being more vigilant. I'd hate to have been one of the passengers in those planes that crashed into the Twin Towers in New York City in 2001. I couldn't help but notice during our Southwest flight, that the kid in front of me was keeping himself busy shooting missiles at a building and scoring points with his game-boy.

Marjorie was so glad to look out from our balcony suite on the Holland America Westerdam. Skies were hazy and overcast. Oh well. But it was nice just "getting away from it all". We were on the cruise! The sun broke out in spurts over Fort Lauderdale as we left port and headed out to sea. I got sea-sick and popped a Bonine and then Gravol and then put the patch behind my ear. Marjorie was fine and started exploring the ship. This was a replay of last year's cruise on the Costa line, where she started giving better directions to people around the ship, than the stewards could.

At supper time, we sat at a table with a fellow who knew all about the motions of a ship. There's rolling, pitching and heaving.

He launched into the definitions of each one of them and indeed, I nearly showed him what heaving was! The captain announced that the swells were 12' high and that the stabilizers were employed. I was thinking, "What stabilizers?"

The boat rocked back and forth, up and down. I didn't care if it was rolling or pitching. I didn't see a distinction. I was just happy for the narrow hallways back to our cabin where I could lay my dizzy head on the bed until I was stabilized. Actually, I didn't heave once and I found reading was a good distraction from my sea-sickness.

That week was the only week I ever out-read Marjorie, notching up 3 books in one week. During our marriage, there had been a dry patch in this endeavour where I did not read one book in 5 years! I'm usually a slower reader anyway absorbing the description of foliage, the architecture and the ambiance before I read whatever the plot is about.

At lunch time, I noticed all the seniors on the ship with canes, trying to acquire their sea legs. There were a fair number of obese people who shouldn't have frequented the buffet as often as they did.

All the Indonesians working on the ship as stewards, kitchen staff and ship crew, were short and skinny. I hoped they paid these people well. I found out they were employed in 10 month stretches to send money back home to Indonesia. Then they took 2 months off. They worked 12 hour days.

When Marjorie got her menu, she observed that the menu wished everybody a Merry Christmas in several languages.

We thought of Canada where it's become politically correct to hear Happy Holidays on TV and over the radio, certainly not Merry Christmas. When we left, the boat rolled, pitched or heaved as we waited by the elevator and an unsteady senior with a cane said: "It takes courage to get old."

There was a station on TV where we could chart the progress of the ship through the Caribbean, with a line and an arrow, showing the different islands we were passing.

The captain announced that San Salvador was just in sight to the left of us. It was discovered by Christopher Columbus in 1492 on his first voyage with the Nina, the Pinta and the Santa Maria, a rhyme that every school child, I'm sure, has had to memorize.

This started it all, colonization, for good or bad. I'm thinking that North American Indians might have wished that Columbus had sailed right by but the real estate of land blocked the way!

It's great that we booked shore excursions for each port: Grand Turk, San Juan, St. Thomas and Half Moon Cay.

CHAPTER 41

———————

Grand Turk reminded me of rubble, lots of stony roads, broken cement blocks at the site of unfinished houses. Everybody builds with blocks and plaster there.

I know Hurricane Ike ripped through there in Sept. 2008 but the place still doesn't look cleaned up. We saw the salt house and the salt ponds where slaves used to work. I sign has been erected outside the salt house, with the slogan: "To be free is very sweet." Below it is a bit of the history of slavery there on the island. Greed and money was behind it all. I was not impressed by our tour guide who seemed disinterested in his job, as he pointed to the left or right in a monotone: Library, Bank, Courthouse. So what?

At least, our tour included a stop at Governor's Beach. I pulled up a lounge chair for Marjorie. I'd donned my swimming trunks and picked up the goggles and fins for snorkeling. That was included in the price of this excursion.

Actually, it was the most fun I had on Grand Turk, sloshing in the water and struggling to get my fins on without sand in them. I finally succeeded and did my snorkeling, retrieving 3 conches from the bottom. I got them on board ship in my old back pack but I didn't realize I'd broken the law because port authorities were confiscating shells and conchs from other tourists who thought they could just walk back to the ship with souvenirs. At night out at sea, I felt so guilty, I took my 3 conchs out on our balcony deck and hurled them one at a time into the rolling ocean. The snorkeling had been fun. I can't say much for the occasional swallow of salt water though.

San Juan was huge, almost ¾ of a million people. Buildings were very Spanish looking and distinct districts in town separated the rich houses from the poor. The business district close to the port had narrow streets with strings of shops: jewelry, clothing and crafts and more jewelry.

We took a 4½ hour trip up the mountain to the El Yunque Rainforest. Maria was an excellent tour guide who explained the buildings we saw on the way, the economy, the gas prices and the government.

Marjorie and I enjoyed the walk along a rocky path through the rain forest once we got there. She even climbed the 98 stairs to the top. Great view of distant mountains, large fronds, ferns, palms and bamboo trees nearby. Fairly overcast the day we were there. There's also a cascading falls further down the winding road where we stopped. Nobody stopped the dare-devil tourist who climbed up the slippery rocks to the foot of the falls for a closer picture. I snapped one of the people snapping pictures of him and got them, him and the falls in, all in one.

Digital cameras are just great. What an era I'm living in! I reviewed my photos sitting on the bus going back down to San Juan. A déjà vu came to me while I was going through the photos and deleting some of them. Somehow, I felt like I'd been here before and had this feeling before. Scientists say it's just a funny trick of the brain. For some reason, at that moment, I wrote a line into the journal I always carried with me: "Will you still love me when I've lost everything?"

I remembered taking Pastor A. to the West Montrose Covered Bridge in St. Jacob's some years ago and using his new digital camera there to show him how it worked.

Pastor A.'s dementia was getting worse and I volunteered twice a month to drive up to Kitchener from Vineland to take him on outings. He had expressed an interest in photography and I used the most basic buttons on the camera to show him how it worked.

I don't know why I thought of that memory from years ago on this ride back to San Juan. I deleted a good dozen photos that were poorer doubles and stared out the window glassy eyed.

Maria, our guide, pointed out the Roberto Clemente Coliseum. The Coliseum is named after baseball hall of famer, Roberto Clemente, who died in a plane crash in 1972, while flying with relief articles to be given to victims of the Nicaragua earthquake. Why did he have to die while on God's mission doing a good deed?

The bus dropped us off in the business district of town just above the port and close to where our ship was docked. Little streets went up hill from the port, all of them full of shops and cars. Evening was creeping up on us. It was getting dark but shoppers were everywhere. Jewelry stores and tobacco shops, row on row, one after the other.

Marjorie was looking for a gold bangle for her sister, Marilyn, for a maximum of $200. We saw bangles with little diamonds priced at $1,100 but the jeweler said that most dealers were getting rid of the lower priced items. Marjorie, in the mean time, also collected gift bracelets from her coupons on the boat and little lucky charms.

The shopping experience was funny. I thought that women had built-in radar as they went from store to store zeroing in on gold like bees to honey. The men stood outside the door holding the bag(s). I was one of them. I took a few pictures of the night-life in San Juan, a bus turning the corner in a busy street, the Christopher Columbus statue in the local square and the little streets with the curio, tobacco and jewelry shops. Then we walked down hill along the cobble-stone streets back to the boat.

St. Thomas reminded me of Grand Turk but on a grander scale. High hills, a sky-lift even (which we couldn't use because of electrical problems), a grand view of the whole island from the top, overlooking orange clay rooftops, white plastered houses and the port in the misty distance with our boat in the distant bay. Carnival's boat was closer. It seemed that the higher you went up the hill in St. Thomas, the richer the houses. Yet I could see rubble and broken blocks where construction was left unfinished.

I felt uneasy with the driver driving on the left side of the road but that's the way they do it there, like in Bermuda. Our black taxi driver had a baritone voice with a rough edge and Marjorie nearly went through the roof when he began to speak on the mic. I was amused with his little ceramic dog, head bopping up and down on his dash. Some people don't think it's very classy, others think it's just plain cute. The driver wasn't as informative as Maria, our San Juan guide, but he did an alright job, which was certainly better than the Grand Turk fellow. By the way, what they mean by a "taxi" in the Caribbean, I found out, is actually a van, not a one car sedan like we have in Canada.

I took a picture of an iguana sitting on the rocks when we first got off the boat, so I got my "wildlife" picture in. From there it was a taxi (van) ride up the mountain for an overview of the bay, orange rooftops from on high and rich people's white villas edged into

200

the mountain side. I got the standard shot of Magen's Bay from a lookout at the side of the road.   Apparently Francis Drake used the bay when he anchored his ship. The bay was donated to the Virgin Islands by Arthur Fairchild in 1943.   Originally the land around it was a sugar plantation and the bay, itself, was named after the daughter of a prominent Dutch family in St. Thomas.

Marjorie figured there were too many stops along the side of the road and too many views of orange rooftops but hey, we got to see the panorama of St. Thomas and Magen's Bay on both sides of the island.

The taxi driver dropped us off again in the business district of town near the port where shops proliferated on both sides of the narrow streets with names like: Captain's Corner Tobacco, and Royal Caribbean Jewelry.   The license plates had a colourful yellow border with a white middle and black numbers. Two black dancers dressed in colourful Caribbean outfits were painted on the left side of the plates, very cheery with the slogan: *Welcome...U.S. Virgin Islands.*

We finally did find "Diamond International" which had a bangle in our price range.   This store made the wait worthwhile while Marjorie weighed which one of the two bangles to get for Marilyn. The head clerk offered me a beer (my first in a year). I thought, "Hey, jewelry shopping isn't so bad!" There's nothing like sipping a cool beer in a jewelry store while the wife grapples with indecisions on which bangle to get. I finally said, "Get the smooth one, it looked shinier." I'm sure my eyes were shiny too by this time.

When the Westerdam shoved off, I appreciated the beauty of the emerald water off the beach but as we got further out to sea, the water turned black. The sky was overcast and hazy and of course, the boat rock 'n rolled. Oh unhappy tummy and unhappy head!

I was glad for the patch and spent several hours in the cabin reading. I'd gone through two books by this time: John Grisham's *The Painted House* and Dan Brown's *Digital Fortress*. When I didn't read, I clicked on the TV, charted our destination on the map on one of the channels and then flicked through other channels to see Tom Cruise in *Top Gun*. I settled for the soccer game: Birmingham against Manchester United. Berbetov had just scored for Manchester giving them a 1-0 lead. Everybody hugged in jubilation. The announcer said that Rooney was still not at his best. His second try hit the goal post. I shut the TV off and went back to reading Dan Brown's *Digital Fortress*.

Half-Moon Cay (pronounced Key) was our last stop, a piece of real-estate that Holland America actually owned, bought for 7 million (I think) to make it their own little island for guests. We booked a glass bottom boat for our tour and enjoyed the informative and perky delivery by our female tour guide.

I got my photos of underwater coral and we simply enjoyed the little boat ride around the bay.

The barbecue wasn't that great. Marjorie had a tough time finding gluten free or dairy free food. We sat on the beach for a while and watched people snorkel and puddle in the azure clear water. Marjorie walked in up to her ankle and kept her hat on to protect her face from sunburn. This was the only clearly sunny day we had on the whole 7 day trip! We were glad to get back on the boat though, after a disappointing barbecue.

Marjorie and I loved the evening entertainment on board the Westerdam, in the Vista Theatre, with truly professional singers and dancers. There was a medley of song and dance from famous Broadway shows, and on another night, we enjoyed the imitation of the Beatles. Really sounded like them too, except "Paul" wore elevator shoes because he was quite short...but really did a great job. I've never seen the Broadway hit, *Rent*, but one particular song touched me deeply (maybe because I've got an introspective soul). It was really sung well. I'd never heard it before and I was so glad I tuned in to the words. My thoughts couldn't help but flash back to Kenny:

> 525,600 minutes, 525,000 moments so dear
> 525,600 minutes how do you measure
> Measure a year
> In daylights, in sunsets, in midnights, in cups of coffee
> In inches, in miles, in laughter, in strife
> In 525,600 minutes - how do you measure a year in the life
> How about love (*Broadway Musical "Rent"*)

As to food in the Lido buffet? And even in the Vista Restaurant? I thought it tasted okay. To me, food is food! But Marjorie was not pleased because Holland America did not have the same gluten free and dairy free choices as we experienced in last year's cruise on the Costa Fortuna. The Costa line gave Marjorie her own special "Maitre di" and her separate menu but with almost as many choices as regular guests had on their menu. I had some of Marjorie's gluten free breads and they tasted good! In fact, there were several varieties of gluten free breads, actually pliable and quite palatable. Gluten free bread usually tastes like cardboard, which unfortunately, it did on the Westerdam.

As to Marjorie's other food on the menu, the chefs simply took all the gluten out of regular meals, so that Marjorie got no sauces, no dressings and ended up with dry chicken or fish or spinach leaves for salad. They simply had no recipes for specifically gluten free meals. We were also told that if Marjorie wanted an extra slice of bread beyond the 2 allowable slices, then we'd have to pay extra! That seemed rather paltry in view of paying several thousand dollars for the cruise.

Seeing four different ports, though, was great. Not having decent gluten free food for Marjorie was not so great. Holland America can take a few lessons from Costa in this regard.   All in all, we're glad we went away for Christmas. Sometimes you just gotta get away from the snow.

CHAPTER 42

Happy New Year
Saturday, January 1, 2011

It's New Year 2011! We're usually in bed by 10 p.m. the night before and then sleep through the midnight hour. We don't party, we don't drink. How boring is that?

I used to get upset when my brother would phone us (years ago) at midnight and wish us a Happy New Year. I asked him not to do that anymore, but to send us a quiet email instead the next day.

Yesterday, on Friday Dec. 31, 2010, we had breakfast on the Westerdam and were the second group to get off the boat by 9:30 a.m. We wished we could have stayed until lunch time but they needed to clean all the cabins for the next group. We waited 9 hours at the airport, couldn't check our baggage until 4 hours before departure, which was supposed to be after 5:30 p.m. The plane was late. So we read and read and read.

I bought Marjorie a little bag of Lay's potato chips (gluten free) for $3.00 (rip off, the bag was tiny). We had a half hour stop-over at Orlando and landed at Buffalo airport after 9 p.m. We didn't get home until after midnight, tired and light-headed. Bed was good. Happy New Year 2011!

Three years previously, we celebrated Christmas 2007 with Kenny at his house. He was so skinny and had only 3 more weeks to live. He made it past New Year 2008 and died on January 18.

Marjorie and I decided that enjoying things was more important for us than saving money. We'd been saving money for years and not really gone anywhere. At that time, in 2008, Marjorie was 51 and I was 62 years old, her with a cane and me with an artificial heart valve and both of us with orthotic footwear.

At the end of 2008, almost a year after Kenny died, we booked our first real exotic holiday away from Canada. It was at an all-inclusive resort, at the Riu Taino, Punta Cana in the Dominican Republic. There is a reason Marjorie prefers taking cruises now after that December in 2008 holiday at the all-inclusive resort in Punta Cana. We had an absolutely horrendous experience at the Riu Taino.

We arrived at midnight and had to search out our little unit on our own with no flashlight. We found that the toilet had overflowed and the room stunk of raw sewage. We went back to the front desk in the dark and had to argue for other accommodations. They said it was only the smell of the ocean. We trudged back and didn't sleep all night. We revisited the front desk early in the morning and finally got relocated.

Marjorie also found that none of the foods at the Riu Taino accommodated her gluten free and dairy free dietary needs, so she resorted to a diet of beans and rice at "the resort." I found a slushy drink which she could slurp down, called a "Banana Mama." But that wasn't worth the $3,500 we paid for this holiday!

And the weather? Oh my! Wind and rain every day, with about two afternoons of sun. We were glad to get home.

But I must say, I met a very pleasant German chap one morning on the beach where I hoped to get a sunrise picture, which I, of course, didn't get. There was no sunrise! I ended up photographing the German fellow instead by a palm tree. We chatted in German for a bit, me with my broken words from what I remember as a kid in Austria.

Jorg Kuehne and his wife, Jana, have been emailing me from Germany ever since. He agreed that the resort was in disrepair, pointing out, what he said, were rat burrows under the buildings around the place. He wasn't charmed by the lack of maintenance.

We were fed up with the idea of a resort, so in December 2009, a year later, Marjorie had me book a Western Caribbean cruise. Thanks to our CAA agent, Layla, the booking went more smoothly than the Riu Taino experience. The ship housed 5,000 people (twice as big as the Westerdam) and the kitchen staff were terrific. This was the Costa Fortuna trip. Marjorie had her own "Maitre di", her own menu and really enjoyed the specific gluten free meals made for her dietary needs. We stopped at Cozumel, Grand Caymen, Ocho Rios and Nassau.

I snorkeled at Cozumel, swallowing salt water and flapping my flippers on the coral reef setting it back about a decade. My guide was not too happy about that and told me to keep my flippers off the coral. I was just glad my artificial valve was up to flopping around in the sea with flippers on the ocean floor, so I could view the colourful fish under water. Great experience, despite an unhappy snorkeling guide!

In Grand Caymen, we took a tour in a glass bottom boat and walked through town. I guess there's a Margaritaville Restaurant and Cafe in just about every island in the Caribbean. Jimmy Buffet is doing quite well with his bar and grill chain and can afford to fly his pontoon plane around the islands. Ah what a life! He won't have to live off sponge cake anymore!

The only disappointment was the Ocho Rios taxi, a van, not really a taxi cab as we know it. The "taxi" took us to Dunn River Falls. The driver took on a paraplegic with a segway and Marjorie with her cane, knowing full well that they couldn't negotiate their way to the upper falls for pick-up.

During the drive up, he said, "Oh by the way, there's an extra $15 charge to get passed a gate into the Falls". He had a rebellion on his hands! We all demanded our money back and that he drive us back to the port immediately. He wanted to take off $10 from each of us for the trip up and back, and we called in the supervisor who profusely apologized, saying the driver should have explained everything that we were getting into when we hired him for a ride up to "see" the Falls.

––––––––––––––––––––

Nassau was interesting, however. We got there in time for their parade, great costumes, floats and marching bands. It reminded me of the Caribana Fest in Toronto. I got great shots of the marching bands, lots of trumpets, tubas and steel drums. I laughed when one of the dancers got close to the tourist barrier, right next to me. Amidst the din, I could make out what he was saying, like a repetitive mantra: "I got a headache. I got a headache."

We also toured *The Atlantis* where Michael Jackson owned the top penthouse which spanned across two structures of the hotel. Michael Jackson apparently once spent a night in the Bridge Suite to the tune of $25,000. Well, now he's dead. We also took a bus tour around Nassau and the driver pointed out the hospital where multi-millionairesse Nicole Smith died. She's gone too. I'm thinking of the Beatle song, "Money can't buy you love."

It also can't buy you health, though pills and good doctors can prolong your life. Queen Elizabeth I said something interesting with her dying words:

> All my possessions for a moment of time.
> ~~ Elizabeth I, Queen of England, d. 1603

Who knows what next year will bring? This year 2010 has brought plenty of good and bad. But I won't worry about it. The New Testament gives us this pearl of wisdom:

> "So don't worry about tomorrow, for tomorrow will bring its own worries."
>   (*Matthew 6:37*)

CHAPTER 43

———————————

Stepping Back for a Moment

Upside down schedule!
Spring 2007

Kenny made his days nights and his nights days. He hated getting up early in the morning and did his creative thinking at night in his basement office where he had his computers and his sound system whenever he recorded a song. He was a workaholic and a night owl.

After Kenny died, Frank Pizzacalla (web designer buddy) scoured through Kenny's computer and assessed, "he's been a very busy boy!" Kenny could not only produce great artistically crafted web sites; he could mass produce them!

Jim Gardner, of the clothing company in Toronto, *Brüzer Built Apparel,* became a special friend of Kenny's, not because Kenny managed the Brüzer web site but because Kenny had an honourable business philosophy which won him respect and the friendship of the business community.

Kenny was serious about serving his customers with not only more service but also more style in the product. He didn't want a stylish office for outside appearances but rather put his style into what counted, for his customers, which was his web sites, real gems in design that won various awards across Canada and Ontario for very creative work.

Kenny expressed his philosophy in his business site **MoreStyle Design Group** (2004-2008):

> More for You
> We don't rent posh downtown office space or have a big shiny boardroom. Nor do we have an exquisitely designed lobby with a smiling receptionist or legions of staff that come in and "punch-the-clock".
>
> What we DO have is a group of experts in their field who truly love what they do and whose only goal is to make you happy. Keeping our overhead and expenses low allows us to give you a lot more for every hard earned dollar you spend.

I kind of wondered about the MoreStyle Design Group. What Group is he talking about?

Kenny was a one-man team and worked incredible hours to gather more clients into his growing business. He, himself, was the one man Design "Group".

Kenny loved web design. He considered slicing up page designs in the Fireworks program as "fun." He designed a personal web site for Dad and hosted it, entitled "blumengarten.com", now "blumentgarten.org" (managed by mc). Kenny also designed personal web sites for his kids. Not every kid can say, "I have my own web site!" Since Darriane was deathly allergic to peanuts, Kenny created a company called "AlertWear.com" which made people aware of peanut allergies. AlertWear.com sold specially designed bracelets for people with allergies of all sorts. Kenny

won the best web design award in the Niagara Region for the year
2007.

Wally and Laura Janzen passed on a Mennonite work-ethic to
their gifted son. With that came other values about the false glitz
and glamour of the world, about hypocrites and "sycophants". He
didn't need "an exquisitely designed lobby" in his business. He
didn't go after "the almighty dollar" and he had no patience with
pretensions. When he worked on his web sites downstairs in his
busy bee office, he listened to modern rock groups who had a
social message about real values, in synch with his own view of
life, about how the world should be and how fake values screwed
things up.

Kenny was pretty well grounded in reality, loving what was honest
and good and hating what was empty and full of lies. In his
office/man-cave, Kenny imbibed the music of groups like *Journey,
Sting, Toto,* and *Econoline Crush,* who sang about hope, dreams,
love, loneliness and the search for lasting values:

> *Momentary fashion, the passing of a phase*
> *Calculated drivel from empty soul parade*
> *Pabulum for the masses, you can't dig the grave*
> *All you ever wanted was a little peace of fame*
> *Oh your lies*

> *Lies* (Econoline Crush "Sycophant" 1995)

CHAPTER 44

_____

When he received that unfair blow in March 2007, that he had lung cancer, Kenny must have gone through mental hell. The physical pains would come later.

Ironically, he had gone to his family physician just for a checkup about a chest cold. At first, they thought he had pneumonia. Nothing more serious showed up on the x-rays but things didn't clear up, so Kenny was sent for CT Scans.

Kenny had no respect for some specialists who sounded highly learned but couldn't say anything definite. He referred to them frustratingly as "these clowns" in one of his posts when nobody could give him a clear answer as to what he actually had and what they could do for him. Time ticked away because the Canadian Medicare System was a "take a number and wait your turn system." Family wanted Kenny to spend the $1,000 and go to the States for an MRI. As a self-employed, businessman, he always wondered where the next dollar was coming from to support the family and pay for bills. Decisions didn't come easy to him at this time when he wasn't feeling very well, health-wise.

Finally, in April 2007, Ken was diagnosed with "*poorly differentiated non-small cell adenocarcinoma*" in his lungs (one of the more aggressive forms of lung cancer). His official 'prognosis' was approximately 6 months, possibly 12 months with chemotherapy and radiation.

As a businessman with a conscience, Kenny told all his clients that he could no longer handle their web sites; he put copies of their sites on CDs and told his people to find another hosting company. He had been "a really busy boy" (as Frank put it later) in building up a business that could pay for the mortgage on his house and provide money for gas, groceries and the bills to run a household, and now...his livelihood was gone. As he got sicker, Kenny said many times to the family, he didn't know what to do because he considered himself the man, the bread-winner.

In the spring of 2007, Kenny went in for a biopsy at the St. Catharines General Hospital. It's ironic that the old General is up for sale now (in 2010). Both Kenny and Marjorie do not have good memories from that hospital about their service and treatment of Niagara patients. A new hospital is currently being built for the Niagara region off 4th Avenue. The new Niagara Health Care Centre will finish construction in 2013 and, according to officials, the happy news is that "the estimated 1,200 or so cancer patients residing in Niagara will no longer need to make the long haul to Hamilton or Toronto for radiation treatment."

If this bigger place is run by the same people that Kenny called "clowns", then we're still in trouble locally! As to Kenny's biopsy in 2007, the surgery went in from the back and Kenny was hurting for weeks from it, and the prognosis was, of course, "lung cancer."

During Kenny's stint at the General, I had problems of my own: my toes were enflamed with gout, so badly that I could not walk! My big toes were purple, swollen and hurt like hell. I got a wheelchair and visited Kenny at the General.

Marjorie had to maneuver me up hill, negotiate bumps, sliding doors, the elevator and long corridors to get to Kenny's room. He called me "gout-boy." I smiled (or smirked).

Kenny wanted to get back home, let his clients know about the biopsy results, close off his business and concentrate on his "Wellness" Blog, his healing and what he hoped would be a miraculous cure, so he could tell these doctors a thing or two about bedside manners and waiting times.

I was restricted to my wheelchair for a couple of months and appreciated Kenny's disabilities and his frustrated anger all the more.

I did a lot of public relations work, unknown to Kenny, that spring and summer to phone and email a bunch of local papers covering the Niagara Peninsula. Some of that effort paid off landing interviews for Kenny so that the public would know his story.

Kenny yearned for supportive comments on his Wellness Blog. I think it became his new passion, since he couldn't pour out his energies into graphics and design work on the computer any longer as a full time job.

In April 2007, Kenny and I had a little misunderstanding about the length of my comments on his Wellness Blog. Having been a former news editor, I tended to be long-winded and use his Blog as a soapbox to sound off about the health care system in Ontario.

Kenny phoned me one day and explained that my comments were getting too long. If I wanted a Blog of my own, he could set one up for me. I was hurt, so I absented myself from his Blog entirely and let other people have their say. I still read it but decided instead to email Kenny directly if I had something to say.

We played email ping-pong for a while. People didn't seem to miss me, except that Kenny finally emailed me back one day and said that I didn't have to quit the Blog entirely.

CHAPTER 45

From: John Hartig
To: Ken Janzen
Sent: May 5, 2007 8:15 PM
Subject: reclining like Josephine

Hi Kenneth:

My wife is reclining this evening on the couch like Napoleon's Josephine (well maybe not her). She's had several coughing fits throughout the day with this bronchitis. Hopefully the medication will kick in soon.

I smiled at Rich's doggerel or "ode" to you and vegetables. He's a creative person. Your musings, by the way, in Saturday's Blog on "Bowling and the Great Purpose" are not unfamiliar to me. I had many questions after a heart-break years ago and after two nervous breakdowns, like you "what kind of life is this anyway!" People need meaning and they need to be appreciated and loved and cared for. That's all I could figure out.

Marjorie just told me today that her great purpose is as an encourager. I believe that, especially during the times when we, meaning me, have had to give things up. The school board is really lucky to have her as a grade 3 teacher because she does two things well: she knows how to teach and she does that as an encourager to kids who really need firmness but firmness with a heart. When I said that I still had not found my great purpose as a

61 year old, she said that I had. I made people comfortable and I could make them laugh.

We are so glad that your little girl, Darriane, had a great time bowling. Kids need to have fun.

Well, it's time to watch TV with my wife. Bronchitis doesn't give her much energy for anything else. She wants me to spend time with her even if it's just watching TV. I'm getting good tips on "Cooking With Julia". Thank goodness, we've got a CSI crime show recorded which we can watch later.

We want you to have an easy and healing sleep tonight though. Kiss the kids, hi to Sue,

John

_____

From: John Hartig
To: Ken Janzen
Sent: May 6, 2007 12:37 PM
Subject: permission?

Ken:

Have I your permission? I'm going to ask my orchestra exec about giving a link on the orchestra website to your Blog. I'm also thinking of giving a link to your Blog myself from my own photography website. And further more, can I forward the Blog link to my dear friends from high-school days?

John

_____

From: John Hartig
To: Ken Janzen
Sent: May 6, 2007 7:40 PM
Subject: link to your Blog is done!

Christine and Scott are very thoughtful to have forwarded "The Serenity Prayer" to you. I've often had to follow this advice:

> **"Living one day at a time**
> **Enjoying one moment at a time"**

Marjorie kissed me on the bald spot in the back of my head. She's going to have a luxurious bubble bath. Her day was better today with that bronchitis, less coughing and less vomiting (pardon the word). She's going to "make me" take a bath after she's done. I hate getting wet in the tub Brrrr. Just when I thought I was primed enough to suit Grizzly Adams, I have to scrub! Oh, just call me Mr. Squeaky Clean.

The link from my website to your Blog is done. Let me know if there are any changes to be made...or if you feel ambitious, you can do that from your end easily enough, I'm sure. I put an image link on both the Favourites Link and the Web Design Pages. And if you notice, I also made a few "minor" changes to my banners and my navigation with the addition of a few pictures. I "saved for the web" from Photoshop but my images are still fairly large, since I wanted to create pictures that would accommodate the larger monitors that people are buying now-a-days.

When I had my nervous breakdown, I also went through a mental fight where I woke up every morning wondering if I wasn't having a nightmare. My salvation was reaching out to God and reading

Psalms. I had no other choice and now, despite the cynicism of intelligent atheists, I don't care. I was weak, now I am stronger.

Marjorie just called me. I need to pick out the daily verse for this evening's devotional. I had better get on to that. Sleep well.

Your brother-in-law,
John

_____

From: Ken Janzen
To: John Hartig
Sent: May 6, 2007 8:00 PM
Subject: link to your Blog is done!

Hey John,

Thanks for all that!! It really means a lot!

You know, you CAN post to the Blog you know - you didn't have to stop completely.

Some of the stuff you just wrote I think would help make people think – well minus the stuff about the "bath" and websites anyway... :)

Cheers Bro!

Ken

CHAPTER 46

———————————

A Penny for My Thoughts?
[hey, pennies don't exist anymore!]

I started adding my penny's worth back on the Blog but I also continued to email Kenny directly. He dubbed me an "old Blogger" as a tease. I emailed him back that very night, who are you calling "old". I wished him a good night's sleep. His counter response was quick:

From: Ken Janzen
To: John Hartig
Sent: May 7, 2007 10:15 PM
Subject: old Blogger

You! Gout-Boy!

Haha :)

Sleep tight back at ya.

Ken (kickin'-cancer's-ass-boy)

———————————

Prayer From The Future
Back At Ya:

Kenny, how I wish you had slept well that night. I know that future nights were not good for you. May it be your presence is out there somewhere in the universe, now and forever, rested and no longer needing sleep. May it be.

May it be an evening star
Shines down upon you
May it be when darkness falls
Your heart will be true
You walk a lonely road
Oh! How far you are from home
   (Enya "Lord of the Rings" 2001)

CHAPTER 47

May 2007

Meanwhile, May 2007 was not a nice month for Kenny who searched to get the best professional help for his lung cancer. He wanted to break out of the local medical bureaucracy in Niagara and go to the bigger centre in Toronto.

He received a phone-call, one day, from a doctor at the Princess Margaret Hospital, saying that an appointment was being set up for him because, "we don't want you to fall through the cracks." Then, for some reason, the appointment was cancelled. I guessed it had been sabotaged because somebody thought there might be a conflict of territorial or medical jurisdiction between Niagara and Toronto. So that door was slammed shut and our hope for a higher level of care was dashed.

Rich Roach was a special friend. He was a grade school teacher, at the time, working at the same school as my wife. He had also played guitar and sung in one of Kenny's earlier bands at one time. Rich took a personal and compassionate interest in what was happening to our family and so he and I struck up an email correspondence.

I emailed Rich after supper on a Tuesday night with the disheartening news about the Princess Margaret Hospital turning Kenny down for review:

From: John Hartig
To: Rich Roach
Sent: Tuesday, May 15, 2007 7:34 PM
Subject: Marjorie and john

Hi Rich:

We don't know if you heard? But the latest news is that we are back at square one, with the Toronto doctors turning Kenny down for further tests. Marjorie was really saddened to hear the news this evening. She needs someone at the school who knows the situation and who understands how she is feeling.

Kenny was so thoughtful. He phoned us himself and explained that he got the bad news at about supper time, 5:30 pm. Kenny is looking to Cleveland and the States for the possibility of further tests.

We are in a difficult time right now. And we need prayer and understanding.

John

_____

From: Rich Roach
To: John Hartig
Sent: Tuesday, May 15, 2007 11:44 PM
Subject: Marjorie and John

Hi, John,

It's late, but I feel it necessary to respond to your heartfelt letter.

This is quite a setback, and it must be very difficult for you and your family. Marjorie is such a beautiful person and it saddens me to think of what she must be going through at this time; but I also know she is proud of her brother's indomitable spirit and loves him more than words can say. When I heard the hope in her voice this morning when we were setting up in the gym, there was a special glint in her eye, that same fire that incites Ken to continue his search into the States for answers.

Marjorie's heart is an ocean, John; it is vast and filled with immortal lodgings for loved ones and those in need. She is adored by her students. Why? Because children can see right through our bodies and read our hearts, even when we do not wish them to.

Prayer and understanding? You got it.

Thank you for letting me know about Ken. If Marjorie should ever need an ear or just some company at school, I hope she knows I will always be there for her. I would love to get her to sing some harmony with me, but only when she is up to it, of course.

Thanks again, John.

Rich

From: John Hartig
To: Rich Roach
Sent: Wednesday, May 16, 2007
Subject: john's say on Medicare

I would like you to know my opinion on Medicare in Ontario. This was too long a commentary to include in my brother-in-law's Blog whom a local oncologist said was dying of lung cancer with only 6 months to live. - jh

_____

CHAPTER 48

─────────────

They Don't Work for Free

Don't get me wrong, there are many wonderful doctors out there but I think, many of them fall victim to being overly busy and to the tight, strict union-like policy of the Ontario Medical Association.

Doctors, of course, don't work for free since the "cap" on their salaries by the government. So now, try making an appointment with a doctor on a Friday afternoon...good luck! In fact a lot of us don't even have a family physician to make any kind of appointment with because of the so-called "doctor shortage" in the province. I feel their union is holding the government hostage and the government is saying, hey we just don't have enough tax dollars to pay these guys the salaries they think they deserve. So a family doctor will have to be content with making only $200,000 a year on a 4 days-a-week job and not $400,000 or more which is what they want.

Like gas prices, all of this seems to be beyond our control. We hear radio ads to voice our opinions on "nomorewaiting.ca" but they want a $20 membership fee to belong to their list.

Doctors through their medical association have launched their own ad to show what genuine, nice professionals they are in their concern over the crumbling Medicare structure. They've come up with 6 Principles posted on "healthiercare.ca" but it's really their Public Relations department that's spun these ideas.

Try writing any complaints to the Ontario Medical Association and see who answers! Well, doctors are self-employed and have to pay their nurses and receptionists out-of-pocket which is why they need higher salaries! Oh? There are two doctors in my community orchestra who drive nicer cars, wear better clothes and live in wealthier parts of town than I do – even at their current salaries for their 4 day a week jobs!

I've read the OMA's 6 Principles and they don't really say anything. They are a fluffy spin, full of generalities aimed at making the doctors of Ontario look and sound good.

> *"We must look to the future, not the past; we must focus on solutions, not problems; we must think about patients and what they need, not what the system can supply."*

Nice political speech from the medical PR department! But if you read behind the words and ask yourself, okay if we must look at what patients need and not what the system can supply, then who will supply what the patients need? That simply means the patients, themselves, will have to supply their own need! That means money and private care. They will have to pay for what the system cannot provide!

Poor people will get crappy treatment and we will have a multi-tiered system like they have in the States, "the land of the free!" There will come a time when you won't be able to get that second opinion or that more skilled treatment unless you have insurance or pay for it out of pocket with your own money.

Well, there goes Universal Healthcare! It's been a nice concept though, over the past 50 years or so, bless that crusty, old Canadian Bible thumper, Tommy Douglas. And who says there's no conspiracy theory out there to take our houses and our savings as we decline into sickness and old age when we don't have the strength any more to fight back! Where in the heck did the idea of a Reverse Mortgage come from? I can't believe the ingenuity of money grabbing companies.

John Hartig

From: Rich Roach
To: John Hartig
Sent: Wednesday, May 16, 2007
Subject: response on Medicare

Hi, John.

It's always good to receive something from you. I share your views on Medicare. When my father was being treated for his prostate cancer, we came to a similar conclusion, watching in horror from the sidelines while we fought for every inch of my father's life. What a mess they made of things. It is not a straightforward business. I often felt one hand didn't know what the other was doing, which is how I feel about Ken's modern medicine men as well.

The money doctors make is scandalous, but what is more aggravating to me is that the needs of the patient are 'not' their main concern. Who go to school for umpteen years to become doctors anyway? What kind of people? What are the motivating factors? I think it starts out with an actual desire to help others, but it transforms into something else as the unions and government get involved. The same thing can be said about the teaching profession. The difference is we don't make that much money - so a teacher 'must' be driven by more noble reasons - like a desire to educate our youth and help bring responsible, self-motivated life-learners into the community.

Enough said.

I am still upset about what happened to Ken today. It really is a rollercoaster, isn't it? And a ghastly one at that. Hope climbs to a crest, like a wave, but we're never sure if it will crash on to a rock or arrive safely on land. Ken's resilience is amazing, and I believe in him.

Oh, I should say how much I enjoyed watching Marjorie's students' rendition of Hamlet. It was a singular pleasure seeing those young boys and girls speaking in Shakespeare's golden language. It was a very proud moment for me as an educator to be in a school where such a thing is possible. She is a special teacher, and I feel so fortunate to be working beside her.

I like your writing, John. Thanks for sharing. See you on the Blog.

Rich

CHAPTER 49

The Family

Kenny still had some meat on his body in spring and through the summer of 2007.

After his biopsy that spring, Kenny and the family took vacation time to go to Myrtle Beach. Kenny wanted to "get away from it all". Lying in the sun, letting his scar from the biopsy heal was a good idea, as was letting his kids play in the sand looking for sand dollars, sea shells and shark's teeth. The problem was he couldn't run away from the sickness which he carried around with him inside of his body. Crossing the border was no escape, not really.

CUSTOMS INTO THE STATES
"Have you anything to declare?"
"Yes, lung cancer."
"Well, it's not an illegal substance, so can get in. Otherwise we'd have to seize it."
"Actually, if you want to seize this, you are most welcome to have it."

CUSTOMS BACK INTO CANADA
"Have you anything to declare?"

"Yes, I've got this burden I'm carrying across the border."

"What it the nature of this burden?"

"Lung cancer."

"Oh, that falls under the foreign disease category."

"But I'm a Canadian citizen?"

"Doesn't matter. There's an excise tax on lung cancer carried back into Canada. There is an exemption application however. You have to fill it out in triplicate! At the wicket over there. Thank you. Next!"

———————————

Anyway, by all accounts, the family enjoyed their holiday at Myrtle Beach. They came back home for round two for their fight against lung cancer, picking up where they left off. Kenny could not escape his own body, no matter how far away he wanted to travel or which border he wanted to cross.

Towards August 2007, Kenny got noticeably thinner. He rode his bicycle out to the local field to watch Darriane at her soccer games. Braeden was strapped into a "bicycle rickshaw" at the back and was tugged along to these games. Braeden would sit with his older cousin Cody, by Auntie Marilyn or Auntie Marjorie and make pucker faces at everybody, hence his moniker, "pucker-boy."

Actually these pucker faces were more like little kissy lips pointed at some adult, which cracked everybody up. Braeden was just turning 2. Kenny would sit in a lawn chair with Sue and say, "that's my boy." He'd cheer his little baby girl on who ran after the ball wherever it went. Five year olds can be funny. They played the game in clusters, chasing the ball like a swarm of bees, now this way, now that way. Nobody played position. If a goal was made, it was mostly by accident. Everybody got a freezie at the end of the game.

At the beginning of Kenny's sickness, Wally Janzen, Ken's dad, got Kenny interested in Chelation since Kenny did not want to go the traditional route of chemo therapy and radiation because of his Epstein-Barr Syndrome. Kenny showed up to some of the treatments but cancelled out on a number of them.

Wally Janzen (dad) invested a lot of money towards finding natural remedies for Kenny in the hopes of curing him. Kenny made faces when he had to drink his shiitake mushroom tea. He bought a sauna at Costco which was assembled in the basement opposite the TV. Cancer cells don't like dry heat. We bought an Apollo goLite for Kenny which was supposed to provide internal sunshine when you plug it in. When Kenny got more bony towards autumn, Marjorie and I bought him a soft sheepskin to sit on. I have it now at the back of my chair facing the computer.

Dad started paying the mortgage for Kenny and Sue way back when Kenny was first diagnosed and had to shut down his business. Dad did that for about 10 months. We paid for Braeden's daycare. Dad also looked into what services were available for a family where the bread-winner was going through cancer.

Actually Kenny's oncologist should have provided all that information for him or had his receptionist do it.

I'm not sure when Kenny had to start morphine but it was very expensive, twice a day, I think, at $150 a pop. Kenny's oncologist at the time did not sign off on the morphine because Kenny did not agree to be part of a trial for traditional chemo and radiation. Kenny wanted to have a *Voice for Choice* to take the naturopathic route. So Kenny had to find a way to pay for his morphine himself.

Kenny also had "Epstein-Barr Syndrome" which was another reason that he did not go for traditional treatment. He realized that chemo would destroy his immune system further, what little there was left of it.

Kenny organized his own fundraiser for Sunday, June 24, 2007 at the Beamsville Secondary School (where he had attended for a while). I dropped off a letter with Kenny's family picture in it, going door to door asking for donations from local businesses. A few of them insisted on their "no soliciting" policy. A few of them actually gave (thank you). Kelly from the Beamsville Health Post donated a box of vitamin supplements and Raymond Blais from the Hyndai Dealership in St. Catharines donated a fancy watch. There were many other businesses who contributed an assortment of items, ranging from a guitar to a golf club to make the silent auction a success. Most of the money went to pay for Kenny's pain drugs which were not covered by OHIP. I was the "official photographer" at the fundraiser, snapping pictures from the set-up to the wrap-up. Kenny was the MC and with his raspy voice and mic in hand schmoozed and chatted with everybody at the event. His arms were so skinny. Ken combined this fundraiser with a CD Release Party. I don't know how many copies of *My Sentiments Exactly* were sold but the CD was a testament to Kenny's great singing voice and to his ability as a composer and musician. Over 600 people dropped in throughout the day. Kids were kept busy thanks to Nancy and Scott who donated their inflatables from *Niagara Inflatables & Games Inc.* The T-shirts, with the slogan, *"I Blog for Hope...I Blog with Ken!"* were also donated by Jim Gardner's clothing company, *Brüzer Apparel.* Obviously Kenny knew a lot of people and had many friends.

He celebrated his 37th birthday on August 5th 2007. He shared that date with Braeden, since Braeden was born on August 5th as well, the little schmoozer stealing the limelight! When Marjorie and I got married back in 1987, we deliberately chose August 5th as our wedding day because Marjorie loved her baby brother so much. When Braeden came along on August 5, 2005, that date meant a triple celebration for the family.

CHAPTER 50

We kept two donations out of the bidding for the fundraiser: two signed copies of Lee Iacocca's book, *Where Have All The Leaders Gone*, published in April 2007, a month after Kenny discovered he had lung cancer.

I originally bought a copy of this well-written book on government corruption and the car industry at Wal-Mart and decided to write the Lee Iacocca Foundation in California, so we could get a signed copy of the book for Kenny's fundraiser, thinking that a signed copy would add to the bidding. In a way, I was naive because a book, even signed by Lee Iacocca doesn't sell as well as a golf club or a guitar.

Anyway, the Foundation secretary sent back not only one but two copies signed by Lee Iacocca personally. On behalf of the Foundation, she wished Kenny well in his battle against cancer. Kenny decided that the books were too valuable to sell off, so we kept them.

From: John Hartig
To: Iacocca Foundation
Sent: Saturday, June 9, 2007 3:34 PM
Subject: Iacocca Foundation Mailing List

Questions: It was really worthwhile to buy Lee Iacocca's book, *Where Have All The Leaders Gone?* It will be an inspiration for my brother-in-law, Ken Janzen, who has lung cancer and has been given 6 months to live. Ken has elected to take the naturopathic route meaning Chelation and supplements.

He is outraged by the same things that irk Lee Iacocca. Ken is a web designer and has created a Blog as a therapy to express what he and his family is going through with his cancer. He also talks about values and priorities a lot and has become an inspiration, himself, to many people in Southern Ontario. Ken expressed anger over the media making a big deal of Paris Hilton's jail problems (in his Blog of June 9, 2007 entitled *Living Vicariously*). I commented on Kenny's posting, making a connection between false Hollywood values and the empty social values addressed in Lee Iacocca's book: *Where Have All The Leaders Gone*? I'm really glad Lee Iacocca wrote this book. You can check Ken Janzen's Blog at this address:

www.thejanzenfamily.com/Blog

It makes for thought-provoking reading.

Sincerely,
John Hartig
(Kenny's brother-in-law)

_____

From: Iacocca Foundation
To: John Hartig
Sent: Saturday, June 9, 2007 6:34 PM
Subject: Iacocca Foundation Mailing List

Dear John:

Thank you so much for contacting us at The Iacocca Foundation. I personally was very touched by your email and added my "2 cents" on your brother-in-laws Blog.

Mr. Iacocca does read every email and letter that is received. He is overwhelmed by the response the book has generated.

With that in mind, we are working on a leadership website. A place where people can find suggestions on what they can personally do as well as a forum for discussion. It should be completed in a couple of months.

Please let Ken know he is in our prayers and to keep fighting the good fight.

Regards,
Norma Saken
Assistant to Lee Iacocca

CHAPTER 51

Autumn Changes 2007

Autumn 2007 was a sad time. Darriane's 6th birthday came up on September 7, 2007 and was celebrated at Granma Shirley's. Kenny was self-conscious about how skinny he looked and he wondered if people would mind. He wore the same shirt to Darriane's 6th birthday party that he was buried in. Jim Gardner from *Brüzer Apparel* took over the barbecuing for the party and Kenny, like usual, sat with different groups, visiting and joking with his clever banter.

I gave Jim my camera and as a result have an amusing picture of Kenny and myself, sitting together, making V signs at the back of each other's heads. I have the *Blog for Hope* T-shirt on in that picture and Kenny has a yellow luau around his neck. The theme for Darriane's birthday party was Hawaiian. Kenny's got that funny little triangular beardling under his lower lip in that picture (which young guys wear), shoulder length hair and wide eyes to make a funny face for the camera. Kenny loved being a ham.

I took a more respectable picture of him and Aunt Irene together
which she later put on her fridge.

*****

Kenny grew skinnier in those autumn months and his internal
turmoil showed. Dad spent more and more money on any and all
possible natural remedies he could. There were boxes of stuff
from expensive health food stores. But somehow, at that stage,
we knew deep down that spending all the money in the world
would not help.

Kenny wrote in his Blog that he wanted to create an association,
Voice for Choice, for cancer sufferers who did not opt for the
traditional chemo and radiation but who wanted alternative
choices for their disease "paid for by the government, just like the
traditional approach". He felt that doctors should be trained in

these alternative treatments. He wanted cancer stricken patients who opted for the natural approach to be able to work with their oncologists and not be castigated for their choice.

He argued passionately that the alternative route should be funded by the system, every bit as much as traditional method. Though this idea, *Voice for Choice,* was expressed in Kenny's Blog as an intention, it fizzled out because he died and the Blog died with him. Canadian doctors are still frowning on natural remedies.

We also wonder if Kenny was not misdiagnosed by local doctors. There is reason to believe he had Hodgkin's Lymphoma. I googled the disease: "The 10-year overall survival rate is more than 90% for early stage (stage I or II) Hodgkin's lymphoma. Since many patients are young, they often live 40 years or more after treatment. Radiation treatments, and some chemotherapy drugs, pose a risk of causing potentially fatal secondary cancers, heart disease, and lung disease 40 or more years later. Modern treatments greatly minimize the chances of these late effects.

Patients with a history of infectious mononucleosis due to Epstein-Barr virus may have an increased risk of Hodgkin's Lymphoma." Kenny had Epstein-Barr and we wondered why local doctors insisted on chemo and radiation and why his condition was not caught at stage I or II? But that's all irrelevant now. Kenny is dead.

*****

Gathered in the kitchen in the autumn of 2007, Kenny was preparing his ugly tasting Shiitake tea while talking with the family. We were sitting around the table and he was at the counter. He insisted that even family could not identify with his plight? He pleaded with us in a frustrated voice: "You don't understand. It's not you!"

We were coming around more often in October and November just to keep company and to help out. Marjorie would make Russian pancakes (ruhrei) for Sue and for Darriane for supper. The pancakes were cut up into pieces in the pan, served on a plate in a heap and then Aunt Jemima syrup was poured on top. They loved it, a good Mennonite dish.

Kenny was usually asleep downstairs on the couch. He did not want to be shuffled off to the hospital. He wanted to be at home with his wife, kids and family around. Kenny was usually asleep downstairs on the couch with pillows and duvet tucked around him so that his bony body wouldn't hurt. Whenever we visited, Braeden, 2 years old at the time, would tell us: "Daddy sleeping." We felt helpless but we were there for him.

We sat or stood in the kitchen talking about this and that one evening. Marjorie was keeping Darriane busy downstairs in the playroom. She and I alternated the job of keeping Darriane busy and away from the adults when they talked. Braeden was usually catered off to Granma Shirley's.

Anyway, our chatting in the kitchen was interrupted by a frightening crash from Darriane's playroom downstairs. Kenny tore around the corner of the kitchen in his bare feet...to see what happened...when he stubbed his little toe on the threshold.

He went down with a wince, a cry and a crash, rocking back and forth in agonizing pain holding his foot. He had broken his toe! I checked downstairs while others attended to Kenny.

A cabinet full of toys had come crashing down onto the floor. Darriane was not hurt; she was just scared by the crash; followed of course, by another crash with her daddy falling in his hurry to see that his little girl wasn't hurt. What a guy! Lung cancer and all, to tear around that corner with the quick instinct of a protective father. And now his toe was broken!

Kenny insisted on getting out of the local Niagara area for his care. He finally got an appointment with the Juravinski in Hamilton but it was already autumn. He had a very painful ride in the van, being all skin and bone, to get to his appointment.

A nurse told him that he should get his papers in order because he was going to die. Things spiraled downhill from there.

I don't know if an idea planted in your head could be the seed to bring about your own fate.

CHAPTER 52

Back To "The Future"
November 23, 2010

I'm still discouraged with the paucity of what we saved from *Ken Janzen's Health and Wellness Blog*. Again I question, like I did time and time before, whether this effort is worthwhile doing even with some of the snippets I copied straight from the Blog?

So far, we've got the titles of the first two Blogs from March 2007: **CT Scans and Surgeons - Oh My!** and **The Saga Continues**.

We've got the two screen captures I took April 27, 2007, **And I Rage** and from December 25, **"The Prodical Son returns this Christmas day!"**

We've got the snippets that I copied in a keepsake folder, thinking these were nuggets worthwhile looking at later.

Finally, we've got the posts that Lois printed out from the later stages of the Blog, none of them from Kenny because he was getting too sick to Blog. Maybe I'm also afraid of revisiting the pain and also at the mountain of work this book would take.

It's difficult to piece together the sequence of comments from Kenny's Blog because the dates run backwards because that's how the pages were printed out. The end of the month came first and then the start of the month came last, if that makes any sense.

I'm the only one in the family who has the time to piece together this big jig-saw puzzle. Sadly, we were only given 22 pages out of 53 pages that Lois originally printed out.

We don't know if the other 31 pages were scrapped by her. We didn't get them. Maybe they just contained people's repeated comments that were insignificant anyway.

Whatever! Our friend Lois handed me 22 pages inside a plastic bag which I eagerly took. I put the bag on a shelf in my study and ignored the contents for months and months, afraid to look at them because emotions were still raw after Kenny's death in January 2008.

There was so much that went missing from all those posts in spring, summer and autumn. I copied some of it but a lot of it went missing after the Blog disappeared.

I can't express how much we would have wanted to preserve so many more of Kenny's own words for the family! Marilyn took over the chore of posting when Kenny felt too ill to write, getting on towards Christmas. For several weeks in the autumn Kenny's voice remained silent.

We all felt that Kenny went in circles with treatments like a little mouse in a maze within the Niagara system. We felt that he would have done better having been sent right away to the Juravinski Clinic in Hamilton or to the Princess Margaret in Toronto.

Kenny was so unhappy with delayed doctors' appointments and tests, and not getting answers, that he "fired" a bunch of local doctors as the weeks went by.

CHAPTER 53

_____

Time Portal To The Past:
Autumn: Kenny Lost Stamina

It looks like when Kenny finally got to go to the Juravinski Clinic in Hamilton, he had conceded to radiation treatments at last, sometime in October. Seven months had already gone by since March when he was first diagnosed. By October 12th Kenny had 5 radiation treatments, though chemo is not mentioned.

We only have a portion of Kenny's October 12th post and then Marilyn, his sister, takes over from there because Kenny just lost his concentration to do any writing himself, being too weak and drugged by all the meds he was taking. We have too, too little of him as written keepsakes.

_____

Here is what I retyped into the computer from what Lois gave us covering those few months from October 2007 to February 2008.

Halfway There
12. October 2007 @ 00:00

Hey All! Just a quick note during a clear moment in my normal fog of pharmaceuticals to let you know that we are halfway done my radiation treatments – 5 done – 5 more to go!!!! It has been quite a ride thus far and I really wish I had more energy to tell you all what has been happening – hopefully soon I will be a little more

like the spunky and energetic Ken you all know and be able to spend a little more time Blogging about my experiences...before I forget
...[portion missing]

Wanting but Can't :(
28. October 2007 @ 20:58

Well people, I am not Ken! I am his sister Marilyn. Kenny so desires to be back to Blogging but does not have the energy or concentration to achieve it, yet! Kenny and Sue are so amazed at the number of people that have continued to comment even when he has not. Your comments, (and poems) warm his heart. Checking the numbers and comments tonight, and the days when he can actually concentrate, brings such a warm smile to both Kenny and Sue.

So thank-you, from them and from the extended family for the out-pouring of your love through your writing.

Now an update on Kenny:
- Radiation has finished as of last Tuesday afternoon.
- He is HUNGRY! Praise God. He has gained over 10 pounds since his radiation has started. He was at 115 lbs but as of tonight, he is 125.5 lbs.
- The Dr's in Hamilton have started him on oral pills. They will eventually wean him off the patch. He has no fat to store the meds from the patches. (You would of thought that his Dr's would of known that from day one.)
- When he is up to it, he goes for a short walk outside with Sue (around the circle). The fresh air does wonders for him.

Please continue to pray for healing, endurance, sleep and the feel of God's loving arms around him and his family.
Marilyn

ps from Ken: thanks SO much Marilyn for pinch Blogging for me!!!!!!!

Each new day is a Gift From GOD!
6. November 2007 @ 21:59

Good evening.
I'm back, stepping in for Ken.
Kenny has asked me to give you the latest update:

- His family MD did a house call this evening.
- He has 2 appointments this Thursday, Nov. 8 in Hamilton.
- The first one is with the Pain Management Dr. at 11:30 am and then at 1:00 pm he has an appointment with the Radiation
- Oncologist. It will be a very long day for him.
- He has some swelling in both legs from the knees down. His sleep could be better. Wishing for that 8 hour shut eye.
- Doesn't seem to be happening yet!

He is enjoying his walks outside with Sue. He did not go out today...a bit too chilly. Where is that beautiful fall weather we were having last week?

Eating.....That seems to be going very well. He has his favourite foods..which Sue always has available.

He feels there is still some lasting effects from the radiation.

Sue says they are living moment by moment, for each new day is a gift from God.

Prayer requests: Endurance to continue with the fight, reduce swelling in legs, peaceful sleep for both Kenny and Sue and the healing touch of God.

Kenny is hoping to be able to Blog himself in the next few days. (we love you Kenny)
Marilyn

Sand Man...where are you?
8. November 2007 @ 22:44

Well, this day was a long one for Kenny and Sue. I went along with them to the cancer clinic for their visits. The first appt. was at 11:30 but they were running behind. So we waited, and waited. Around 12:30ish we were ushered into a room. The pain management nurse is great. She jokes around with Kenny and he right back at her. The pain management Dr. came in about ½ hour later. Kenny has not been sleeping well the last few nights/days, plus he has severe lower back pain that goes away instantly when he is in the tub. The Dr. thought that it is muscle related. The muscle must be inflamed for some reason. So some new meds have now been prescribed to help with that. From there we were sent down to see the radiation oncologist (who also could not be nicer). He informed us that the radiation still works on the tumor for a few months after. We were happy with that little bit of information. Both Dr.'s want to see Kenny again in 1 month. The hospital staff that Kenny sees are top notch.

I could not ask for anyone better or more caring for my brother.
Prayer list:
1) Sleep. He needs sleep so badly.

2) lower back pain is overpowering
3) Endurance to keep fighting this fight
4) the healing touch of God!
5) Please also pray for Sue.
Thanks
Marilyn

John 14:27
"Peace I leave with you; my peace I give you. I do not give to you as the world gives. Do not let your hearts be troubled and do not be afraid."
12. November 2007 @ 21:30

An Update:
1) HE STILL HAS SEVERE LOWER BACK PAIN.
-he is using a heating pad when resting.
-the pain comes in waves.
-the meds do not seem to be helping
-it is so difficult to watch when a wave hits.
2) SLEEP IS STILL A PROBLEM.
-I think his nights and days are mixed up.
-he sleeps better during the day than at night.
-his body is craving sleep
3) TRYING TO STAY POSITIVE.
-when in pain....being positive does not come easily.
4) FEET ARE STILL SWOLLEN.
-Marjorie has brought him a foot spa/massager.
Hopefully it will provide some warmth and help with his circulation. ☺
My updates do not change much. ☹ Please continue to pray for Kenny, Sue, Darriane and Braeden.

Thanks
Marilyn

_____

Small Miracles Do Happen!
17. November 2007 @ 22:41

Well, Jerry and I visited Kenny, Sue, Darriane and Braeden this afternoon. Kenny was up walking around his family room when we got there. We sat down to listen to a DVD of "JOURNEY" from 1981. Kenny's type of music. One question we were wondering about is, "Did they perm their hair or was that natural?" It WAS 1981 you know. John Gortson had come for a visit this morning which Kenny really appreciated.

Thanks John!

Kenny had a strawberry jam sandwich while we were there. He was hungry. We brought him Lakota roll on Gel for his lower back pain. Sue put some on him and we waited to see if it had any effect on his pain. He feels that his lower back was not so tense nor as stiff as before. Maybe it will work. Let's pray something does.

This past week Kenny has witnessed God's miracles. Maybe not the BIG one we all want but some others. One was: He was walking the floor one night, and telling Sue that he needs some slippers for his cold feet. The next morning, outside their front door was a pair of blue slippers. Just has size. Our aunt Irene felt she needed to give Kenny some slippers. WOW! The second answer was: His swelling in his legs and feet has gone down. Another WOW and THANKYOU GOD!!!!!!! There are some others, and Kenny wants to thank you VERY much. (You know who you are)

"God please keep showing Kenny and Sue you are with them!"
I had asked Kenny if there was anything specific that he would like me to post. He told me to tell you he feels a wee bit better.

He is thanking God everyday for his love that he continues to show to his family and him.
Marilyn

_____

living IN the moment!
20. November 2007 @ 07:37

Last night I called Sue to ask how their day went. I was happy to hear, "GOOD, the day was actually a good one!"
Music to my ears.

Kim and Craig (friends/family) came over in the late morning for a visit. Kenny was feeling okay, enough to want to go out for brunch. WOW.

They went to a buffet in Niagara Falls, sat at a window seat and enjoyed the outing. Being out with friends, breathing in our great Niagara air & feeling the cold wind on his face did wonders for his mind. The last few weeks, he has been stuck indoors. His whole being soaked in the moments of being alive. He was LIVING IN THE MOMENT. When these great moments come his way he needs to grasp them. I do have to admit that he had his painful moments throughout the day...he was not pain free. Our father came over for a visit in the late afternoon. Another blessed time, spending time with the father you love. Overall a very good day. Sometimes it feels like one good day is followed by 3 bad days. Please pray that this is the start of more good days than bad. If Kenny has a good day....we all know that Sue has a GREAT day. So everyone's prayers were answered for a better day for Kenny yesterday. THANKS.

Each day I hope that when I turn my computer on, Kenny would have Blogged himself. Hopefully one day soon, Kenny will be Blogging again.
But thanks for listening to me and praying with me.

CHAPTER 54

John's Blog Comment
Unknown Date and Time

Dayna Stratten included a touching poem which feeds the soul. What a lovely line: "I wish you the sunshine of tomorrow." This is a wish for you, Sue, and the rest of the family, indeed all those who are part of this Blog! People need to be fed by poetry and by the empathetic spirit of others. But then, people also need to be fed by the practical side from family and friends who give a helping hand.

Marjorie and I were glad to have dropped in last Saturday. We got hugs from Braeden and Darriane which are always treasured gifts of affection to us. We also saw Craig and Kim Frere in action. Craig replaced the fluorescent lamps in the garage and got the lights to work, a thing which needed doing. Kim made French toast in the kitchen for everybody. I mounted a picture on the wall in Braeden's room of Kenny reading to his little tyke. Marjorie is willing to help again with more of the government paperwork and forms that have to be filled out. She's so logical and great at details, that it's a wonder she ever married me! Maybe it's the fact that I'm a Brad Pitt look alike (or I'd like to be)! I hear that Craig Frere also gets mistaken for Brad Pitt himself on occasion.

It's niiippppy today. Hopefully this note will warm you up. Consider it also a "rain check" or a "snow check" for Marjorie and myself to make supper for you and the kids again later this week. Just let us know when you want to cash in on it. I make a great chili that is the rave of Vineland! Also if you have a door knob that needs fixing or drippy faucet (or whatever), I'm just a phone call away and only a 20 minute drive.

Marjorie and I are praying that you keep getting fed by the poetry and warm spirit of family and friends and that you also get help from the practical side too to keep house and home together. "I wish you the sunshine of tomorrow."

Squishy hugs to Braeden and Darriane
Uncle John and Aunt Marjorie

CHAPTER 55

———————

Thinking CHRISTmas
28. November 2007 @ 07:32

Well, Christmas is just around the corner and Darriane's tree is up and lit in her bedroom. She has a small white tree with red decorations.

Braeden loves the PRETTY tree.

We sat in their family room last night talking about Christmas and when we should have it. Planning a tomorrow is good. Everybody lives close by except my daughter and her husband so we usually plan the day around their schedule.

Talking about Christmas made the evening seem "almost normal." Kenny told us that he had a very bad day yesterday. Out of 10, the pain was 8. He has never had a day like that before. He cried out to GOD many times yesterday, but felt that God was so far away.

Marjorie and John had Darriane for the weekend and had brought her to church. Darriane went to Junior church and the lesson was on God's Healing Miracles. That was a very difficult lesson for a 6 year old to understand. Here this teacher tells her that God cares and actually has healed many people. WHAT ABOUT DARRIANE'S

DADDY? Please pray for Darriane that she CAN feel God's LOVING arms around her and her family.

She sees all and hears all. Her mind is so confused with what she sees and with what people tell her.

Our Aunt Irene brought over supper last night for the family which was enjoyed by them all. Darriane did need "flavouring" on her noodles though. Braeden devoured his food, just like his daddy used to do.

Kenny's swelling is back in his legs, and his appetite is not as good as it was. Please do not forget this family in prayer this Christmas season.

Marilyn

John's Retrospective on November

Kenny's strength failed him through November. That was a difficult month.

Sue got him a walker so he could exercise his legs downstairs where more and more family gatherings took place because he couldn't come up the stairs to the kitchen. For those of us who got coffee in the kitchen, we could still see Kenny downstairs because of the split level floors separated by a spindled railing. Kenny would walk in circles in his bathrobe and slippers, using the walker. I called it his Indy 500. I bent over to him one time when he was doing his Indy 500 and whispered to him that I wished I could have been of more service to him in his business. "That's okay," is all he said. I would have worked for free in his Web Design business, just as a learning experience, because he knew so much about computers. But when he was healthy, he was like a Formula 1 race car fueled on nitro, ready to get to the finish line first.

When Kenny did his Indy 500, he occasionally played with the remote to see what was on TV. He liked the hockey games. I asked if Sydney Crosby was really that good. Kenny said, "Yes!"

Kenny's other favourite show was *Extreme Makeover* with Ty Pennington. He loved the *Simpsons*. And to my surprise, he occasionally watched *The Raccoons*, one of my favourite cartoons, with Burt Raccoon, Cyril, the Aardvark, and the other animals in the Evergreen Forest.

Kenny still made it upstairs, with effort, into the bathtub to ease his aches with a good Tom Clancy novel.

At one point he was confined to the couch and the remote was out of reach. He whispered to me, in a raspy voice, about a little button to press on the stereo. I couldn't see the button. He drew a picture and I still couldn't see it. Through his anger, his raspy voice muttered, "Jesus Christ!" and he forced himself up and staggered over to press that little button himself. I'm sorry about that Kenny. "I muffed it."

I'm not sure whether it was November or December when Kenny had "Danny Z" come over to be a witness to his will. Danny Z was a professional magician, a special friend of Kenny's. Danny cried as he signed the papers in duplicate, triplicate or whatever he had to sign. It was touching and sober.

Kenny had edema. His feet ached all the time and were swollen like balloons right up to the ankles and calves. I could relate with the gout I had some months back. Family took turns massaging his feet. I took on that chore too, willingly.

Kenny had trouble swallowing regular food so he could not get anything substantial into his stomach. We brought him *Coffee Crisp* chocolate bars and ice cream bars because that seemed to be the only things he could keep down and keep his weight up, the little he had. By Christmas he must have weighed under 100 pounds. We knew that cancer loved sugar but we didn't know what else to do to keep Kenny's weight up.

Marjorie volunteered to make Mennonite "ruhrei" (chopped up crepes) for the kids and Sue to keep them going during late autumn. Darriane, especially, just gobbled the pancakes up with syrup.

Jim Gardner visited in late autumn and brought sandwiches for the family. He wasn't just a client of Kenny's, for whom Kenny did the *Brüzer Apparel* web site, a great success story in Toronto, but Jim had become a special friend because of Kenny's charismatic personality and honest business ethics. We appreciated Jim's thoughtfulness in bringing us food when the family was too depressed to think about that. We were also grateful to Aunt Irene, a retired head nurse, who came to the house and helped Sue with administering to Kenny.

CHAPTER 56

Marilyn Pinch-hitting Again

Just you and me.
5. December 2007 @ 07:36

So here we are again......just you and me.
Well, for the people that do not get my father's emails this is the updated version.

Kenny was to go to the cancer clinic this past Monday afternoon. He felt he was too weak to travel there and back PLUS having to lie down on the mat for his scan would have been too painful. They have postponed it to Dec. 20/07.

Wow, just before Christmas!
This Thursday...Dec. 6, he is to be back at the clinic to see the pain management DR plus to see the radiologist oncologist.

This appointment had been booked 4 weeks ago. They were also going to go over the results of the body scan done this past Monday. We will see if the appointment still stands for Thursday and how Kenny is doing also. Kenny has been very weak for the past few days. His blood pressure has dropped some (not by much). His heart was racing yesterday. Anxiety?

Still having trouble sleeping. His pain does not seem to be able to be put under control. Now that is the biggest problem.

The Sauna is down in the family room and the Christmas tree is up. Another thing done to get ready for Christmas.

This past Thursday, Kenny's and Sue's china cabinet fell over and (you've guessed it), everything broke. The top part of the cabinet was screwed to the wall. It has been there for years. Kenny thought that someone had driven through their living room window, for the crash was way too loud. "Thank you God that nobody was in the dining room at the time!"

Sue is a bit under the weather. Starting with a tickle/cough. That is all she needs on top of everything else.

ps...if you come across some gibberish in the comments...please do not open them up to see what they are. Some people get enjoyment out of doing stupid things. [Those are malicious links.] I will try to delete them as I see them. (hopefully before you do).
The Medical Mystery that is Me :) | Comments (436)

CHAPTER 57

_____

John's Nickel's Worth
No More Pennies Due to Inflation!

Cancer hates heat. We were glad that Kenny bought the sauna from Costco and had it installed downstairs in the family room. We were also glad that the Christmas tree was put up in the living room. We had hopes that Kenny could have yet another Christmas with us. But somehow negative things kept piling up unasked. Sometimes it doesn't just rain, it pours.

The china cabinet fell off the wall shearing parts of the the wall down with it. Sue got a sore throat. And then the Blog was sabotaged by porn malware. Hundreds of unwanted links poured into the comment boxes. Usually, regular comments ranged from 20 – 50 on a given day. December 5, as you see, comments numbered 436, most of them gibberish with links to porn sites. We felt violated and there was nothing we could do about it.

I'm not sure if anybody bothered Kenny with the problem. He wasn't in any shape to deal with it, even though he was the computer expert in the family. Marilyn did her best to delete as much of the garbage as she could. She hoped that her warning came in time so friends and family would ignore the unwanted links. The fact that this happened at all in Kenny's Blog underscores the fact that there are some really mean people out there, to dump porno links into the Blog of a cancer victim.

Kenny felt utterly weak and helpless in December. I'm not sure if it was at this stage when he asked his dad, "Do you still want me around?" He was concerned about the trouble he was causing the family, imagine that? He was concerned about us when we were all concerned about him.

A young pastor spoke at St. Ann's Community Church one Sunday morning, recalling a canoe trip with his dad when he was a kid about 12 years old. They ran into a storm halfway across the lake. They got drenched and cold, paddling in the rain and the wind. The dad threw out encouraging comments to keep his son going as they laboriously made headway toward the distant shore: "I love you buddy, we're almost there. I know the way."

Years later, the pastor came up with this prayer that he passed along to his church, whenever he told his story, which I passed on to Kenny's Blog:

> May the Creator of the Universe
> hold you tight and say
> that He loves you
> and that we're going to make it.
>
> I love you buddy, we're almost there.
> I know the way.

CHAPTER 58

Marilyn's Comment about Needing Sleep!
6. December 2007 @ 16:54

Well, I hate to be the bearer of bad news, but we did not go to the cancer clinic today. Kenny had a very bad night plus he was in alot of pain this morning. He was too weak to make the drive. Please pray for a peaceful sleep tonight for both Kenny and Sue. Marilyn

The Medical Mystery that is Me :) | Comments (35)

Everybody needs an Aunt Irene!
11. December 2007 @ 18:02

Well, some of you have received an email from our father. I thought I should also write to you in case you do not receive his mail personally.

This past week-end was very difficult for Kenny. He was in severe pain constantly. He was asking Sue to help him. She asked if she could call the ambulance for him. The answer was NO! "I am not going to die in the hospital, but at home!" Sue called the pain management nurse for help. She suggested raising his meds, but it would effect him mentally. He is not in much pain anymore but he is now hallucinating, and it is getting worse. John, Marjorie, Jerry and I went last night to be there for Sue and Kenny. It was very difficult to sit and watch our brother. He tried so hard to stay focused. He does not like being like this but it helps with the pain. Now, we have an Aunt Irene who is a treasure. She offered her services to Sue and Kenny for last night. Aunt Irene and Sue took turns sitting with Kenny. Shirley has taken Braeden and Ray has taken Darriane.

Kenny fell this morning, and Sue was so thankful that Aunt Irene was there to help pick him up. Our Aunt Irene was a nurse at WLMH until she retired, then went into organizing palliative care in the Niagara Region. (hopefully I have that correct) She is perfect for taking care of Kenny and Sue. Sue's burden of being alone at night has been lifted. Thank you God for this answered prayer.
My father's sister-in-law (Aunt Agnes Janzen) passed away this morning. She was 93 years young. Death seems to be around too many corners, peaking out at us.

"God hold us close, for our hearts are breaking."
Marilyn
The Medical Mystery that is Me :) | Comments (63)

_____

Climbing out of the valley!
16. December 2007 @ 11:43

Well, this week feels like it has been a month. Sue has been a "wonder woman" as Aunt Irene has labeled her. Sue has been surviving on minimal sleep but you wouldn't know it. Here is how the week played out at Kenny and Sue's house: Aunt Irene stayed from Monday evening until Friday at noon. Every evening, John, Marjorie, Jerry and myself came over to give some comic relief (to help support, encourage & love). Shirley had Braeden for the week. Friday at noon, Shirley came over to relieve Aunt Irene (so she could go out with friends to Toronto). Then Marjorie and John came over to visit around 2:30ish so Shirley left. Dad and Judy brought supper around 5ish for the family. Marjorie and John took Darriane home with them for the week-end. I went over to Kenny and Sue's around 10:15ish to stay the night. Kenny slept very well Friday night. His hallucinations seem to have stopped. He was also having jerky movements, which have also stopped. (PRAISE GOD!)

His pain seems to be finally managed. (after how many months?) Jim Gardner (from Brüzer-Toronto) came over with his son Saturday afternoon, with some Christmas Gifts from his family and his extended family.

Jim, you know you are loved by the Janzen family. Thank you.

Andrew (my youngest son) went over last night to watch a movie with his favourite uncle. He stayed the night and both were still sleeping when I talked to Sue this morning. Sue said they had another good night. Hopefully we are climbing out of the valley. A great B I G Thank you to all of you for praying for Kenny and Sue this week.

God's loving arms were felt by all of us. With Christmas upon us, my prayer is that Kenny will be feeling well enough to enjoy every moment with his family.
So far it is looking good. ☺

UPDATE...Dec. 18

Kenny has been in a lot of pain again. One day he seems to be pain free and then the next "wham" it hits him hard. They are upping his meds again. Sue has been placing a heating pad on his back to try to lessen it somewhat.

Sue was told Sunday that her cousin Tim (32 years old) died of a heart attack. He lives in Toronto. The memorial/funeral will be this week. Life hits hard sometimes, and it is worse when we are already down.

Marilyn

The Medical Mystery that is Me :) | Comments (29)

CHAPTER 59

Re: Climbing out of the valley!
Comment By John and Marjorie
18. December 2007 @ 00:47

Marjorie and I feel helpless too. Marjorie shed tears this evening wanting her baby brother to feel less pain. Less pain would be a good day. Dratted disease! I refrain from using stronger words. That won't help our helplessness.

Aunt Irene was a real trooper last week for staying overnight at Kenny's to be a burden bearer there with Sue. She slept better the second night when Marjorie suggested removing the cushions from the couch to make more elbow room. Her nursing experience has come in handy at the house and Sue just appreciated having another adult there to lend a helping hand.

Marjorie and I kept Darriane busy over the weekend with horseback riding at Olive and Elsa's barn, bowling in the afternoon and the real-live re-enactment of the Evening in Bethlehem at the Calvary Gospel Church in Beamsville (donkeys and sheep and all). Darriane even helped to shovel snow on Sunday during the blizzard. When it let off somewhat we wanted to be ready to drive Darriane home to her mommy whom she was sorely missing.

We had a stressful time driving 60 km along the QEW but we actually made it onto Vine Street near Kenny's. Alas our Elantra was not a Jeep, the side-roads there had not been ploughed yet into Cindy and Beau Valley. We left the car in a clear spot on Vine and then trekked with Darriane's overnight packs through the ruts and ridges and the blowing snow for about 1 km until we got to Kenny's House. Sue was so glad to see her little girl. Darriane was a real trooper for having trudged that whole long distance in the blowing snow. Imagine a six year old! Aunt Marjorie kept calling out "another stop sign, only a little bit further to go. We're almost there."

Marjorie and I were glad to get Sue's little girl back home safely. She was also glad to see her big cousin Andrew at the house (Andrew's about 6'4" 😵. They're real buddies. Marjorie and I trudged back to our car through the ruts and headed back home "extremely carefully". We felt calmness replace the tension when we pulled into our very own driveway. Darriane was home and so were we.

Kenny, Kenny, I wish I could wish you better...maybe my little prayer tonight might help just a bit.

Marjorie loves you so much...and I'm so pleased to be your brother-in-law.

Sleep, sleep, let the pain go away, God Grant Us Peace.
John and Marjorie

Re: Climbing out of the valley!
By Ed Warneck – Myrtle Beach, SC
18. December 2007 @ 05:59

Ken and Sue... I am pleased reading that Ken has been blessed with some relief from his suffering. It has been a tough journey for the Janzen family. So it is heart warming to all of us who pray for you and your family in your time of need.

It is equally comforting to me that you never waiver with your strong faith and love for our creator. Never once, have I heard the words "why me", instead you pray for those around you.

Ken, when my daughter laid in a comma for months, and hope was painted as slim to none by most that she would survive, I never understood the "why" tragedy hit her. I struggled with this everyday while I sat by her side waiting for a finger to move, an eye to open, anything at all to give me hope. Like me, I am sure all your loved ones pray moment to moment for your situation to improve, a sign to be given that our prayers were being heard.

We hold onto faith and our belief that our Lord is a merciful yet we bend and weaken at the knees at times when we don't understand his plan.

Each day when I would leave her bedside to use the restroom, or grab a bite of a sandwich, or say thanks to the hundreds of people and students who camped in the hospital lobby for weeks on end,

I would pray not for things to get better, but rather for things to remain the same until I returned.

One day as I walked down the hall to the return to the trauma center reciting my usual prayer asking God to allow things to be as they were when I left, I heard a voice or maybe it was just a thought, but nevertheless it was his words that said to me
if you trust in me, you don't need to ask.

It was at that moment when I truly understood that just my prayers, but all our prayers are heard.

Over the next few days I took stock of my inventory and wondered was there a sign I missed and then I realized that our Lord reveals himself to us through family, friends, and yes ... even strangers you might otherwise never pay attention to. He lives in all us all the time and reveals himself through their love, kind words and deeds.

Look into the eyes of those around you and you will know he is with you and your family every minute.

We will never understand the why.

But it is his plan, for whatever reason, you are traveling this difficult journey at this time. It is his plan, including myself, that we travel this journey with you. However, please keep in mind, no matter how difficult it gets at times, he holds you in his arms and will never let you go.

I think of you often and pray for your comfort and recovery. I pray for Susan and your children and all who surround you. You and Susan are truly admired by all who know you. God is pleased with you both.

And so my Canadian friend, fear not. I wish you and your family a Blessed and Peaceful Christmas. I look forward to seeing you and your family here on vacation this coming spring.

May the grace of God be with you always....

Ed Warneck and Erika , Myrtle Beach

PS - As you know, my daughter Erika who had no chance, greeted you in our office when you stopped in to see us. She is another example that prayers are heard. She asks about you often.

I'm sure you are in her prayers too.

CHAPTER 60

A father's words!
20. December 2007 @ 18:47
Dear Friends of Kenneth and Sue:

You may recall that several weeks ago Kenneth was scheduled to have a CT scan but didn't go because of feeling weak, etc. The scan was postponed until today but again they decided not to go which makes a great deal of sense to me. Kenneth is so drugged with morphine, hasn't slept for quite some time, hasn't really eaten much of anything, and is much too weak to make the long trek to Hamilton. Several months ago the doctors told Kenneth and Sue that they would make that gradual change from morphine to methadone (it can't be done in one session) because the morphine poses too many side-effects it shuts down the bodily functions. Nothing was done for quite some time and now that his pain has surfaced again the only option is to give him more morphine. Kenneth rarely speaks and when he does it is in the form of a whisper. I believe he just doesn't have sufficient energy left to communicate.

Kenneth asked that we all meet at his house for our family Christmas dinner this coming Sunday. We are hoping and praying that he will be there with us to enjoy meeting some of the family who live at some distance and who haven't been able to see him and Sue as well as their little cousins as often as they would like. Over the years I have come to realize what a charismatic

274

personality Kenneth has.   His charm is so infectious and is evidenced by the many, many friends he made.

His Blog and individual emails directed to me have told me time and again how much he is loved by so many.

Sue read Ed Warneck's Blog comments to him. When I asked him whether he knew that Ed had commented, a great big smile crossed his face. This was sufficient proof how much he had appreciated your words, Ed.

I find it extremely difficult to think that God knows best in all instances and especially for my son. He is loved so dearly by the family, and his immediate family needs him so very much. I have read all the prayers that you have posted on his Blog and it appears that God chooses to answer as He chooses. (The pot does NOT dictate to the Potter how it is to be made and what its function is and how long it is to be used-I realize that I am selfish and only want what I think is best for my son whom I love so dearly.)

In the months that Kenneth has had to endure his illness, he has never really complained. Had he had the stamina he would have told all of you repeatedly how much you have meant to him, how much your comments on this Blog have provided emotional support for him and his extended family. Sue has had a heavy load to bear over these months as you can well imagine. Please continue to pray for Kenneth, Sue, Darriane and Braeden.

Thank you to all who have been so supportive, empathetic and compassionate.
Sincerely,
Wally (dad)

Re: A father's words!
By Marjorie
22. December 2007 @ 18:13

It's been quite awhile since I last posted. John keeps up with the Blog but I find it too hard to read and I end up sobbing. John showed me Dad's letter tonight as I was wrapping Christmas presents for Darriane and Braeden and after the tears dried I reached for my Bible and opened it to a passage that I have underlined and have read many, many times this year. It's Psalm 42, specifically verse 11.

Why am I discouraged? Why so sad? I will put my hope in God! I will praise him again - my Savior and my God!

Medicine cannot cure Kenny, doctors seem unable to help much, there's nothing we can do but pray and be there for Kenny and our family. Only God can change the situation. It's in His Hands.

Kenny, Sue, Darriane and Braeden, you are all so special to us. We love you so! We continue to pray!

Marjorie

Re: A father's words!
By Alma
23. December 2007 @ 19:59

Isaiah says...."Do not be afraid, for I have ransomed you, I have called you by name; you are mine. When you go through deep waters and great trouble, I will be with you. When you go through rivers of difficulty, you will not drown! When you walk through the fire of oppression, you will not be burned up; the flames will not consume you. For I am the Lord, your God, the Holy One of Israel, your Saviour. Isaiah 43:1-3 and verse 4b says ...you are precious to Me, you are honored, and I love you.

vs. 5 says...Do not be afraid, for I am with you.
I too, want to covenant to pray specifically for all of you on Dec. 24 at 10:00pm Eastern time.

Alma

CHAPTER 61

Family Christmas
By Marilyn
24. December 2007 @ 14:42

Yesterday was a very special day for the Janzen family. We were almost all there. Wally (dad), Judy (stepmom), Marjorie and John, Jerry and myself, Tamara and Jordan (from Barrie), Andrew was there for a short time (he had a temp. and did not feel well) were all present, but my son Shaun (Kenny's oldest nephew) was not able to have yesterday off from work, but his wife Rachael and baby Ethan (5 months old) were there.

When we started in the afternoon, Kenny was sleeping. We all gathered around Kenny in the family room and dad gave the prayer for our food, but also for our loved one who was suffering. The prayer brought tears to our eyes, for we so wanted a different Christmas. Darriane held Sue as the tears flowed. That by itself brought more tears to our eyes. We were not too sure if Kenny knew that we were even there. By the time we had finished our main course, Kenny presented himself upstairs. Wow, now the celebration started. Kenny and Sue watched Darriane and Braeden open ALL their gifts from our family. More & more gifts just kept showing up. Kenny sat so quietly watching with a smile only a father gives for his children. After the children had opened their gifts, we adults played a game. We each brought a $15.00 gift wrapped up. We picked a number and the person with #1 went first. The #1 person got to pick any present but the best part is that they also got to go last. Kenny happened to pick #1.

It was not rigged. Honest.

After Kenny picked, #2 person could take away Kenny's gift or pick one not opened, and so on...After everyone has picked, #1 person (Kenny) got to look at all the gifts opened in our laps and if he so chooses, he could exchange his gift for it, and then the game was over. It is a very fun game and we all enjoyed it. Dessert was still to be had. Kenny said he felt he needed to go lie down but he did not leave. He stayed upstairs with us till we all left to go home to our beds. A lot of tears were shed last night. Our memories are very raw most days. Tears are not very far from the surface. When I called Sue this morning at 10:10, Braeden was STILL sleeping. We tired him out last night. Kenny had his normal sleeping last night (bits here and there). He was still very tired this morning. He pushed himself last night. I have to be honest, WE needed him with us last night. (for us, Sue and the children) Our family thanks God for allowing the special time of yesterday to happen. We felt your prayers throughout the day and evening. That is how Kenny was able to be part of our family celebration. We know that our family is not the only family suffering this Christmas.

Please forgive us if we seem selfish.
Today should be a quiet day for Kenny. Hopefully he can sleep a peaceful sleep.
Tomorrow, (Christmas day) Sue's side is getting together. The meal will be at Shirley's and John's and then the family is going over to Kenny and Sue's to open gifts with them.

Please keep tomorrow in your prayers. Sue's side needs a celebration tomorrow also.
Thursday (Dec 27) Kenny has an appointment in Hamilton to see the Dr.'s.

Stephanie....thank you for letting our Blogger family know about your idea. The prayer for Kenny at 10:00 tonight sounds great. Thank you to all for praying for our family & we hope you have a Merry Christmas.
Marilyn
The Medical Mystery that is Me :) | Comments (13)

CHAPTER 62

John's Reflection

We were grateful, as a family, to have had Christmas at Kenny's house for the last time on the evening of December 23, 2007: Kenny, Sue, Braeden, Darriane, Wally (dad), Marjorie (sister), myself, Marilyn (sister), Jerry, Tamara (Kenny's niece), Jordan, Andrew (nephew), Shaun (nephew), Rachel and baby Ethan. We opened presents on this sad occasion trying to be happy. Kenny gave dad a Gilligan's hat for Christmas.

I did Photoshop magic later on my computer inserting Kenny into the picture beside dad where he tipped his Gilligan's hat to the camera.

Darriane held Ethan like a little mom and teased him with a toy. Braeden put a soup bowl on his head being a ham like his dad. The kids romped around with Jordan (the body builder in the family) and Kenny looked on taking in the family antics with a smile. He opened Christmas cards and cried. I took pictures and stopped when Kenny complained that the light of the flash was hurting his eyes. Kenny was gaunt and pale. It hurt to put on a happy face for him.

CHAPTER 63

Kenny's Christmas Post

Kenny rallied enough on Christmas morning to actually post something on his Wellness Blog. The spelling errors and rambling thoughts showed a tired mind, just plain tuckered out with the battle.

The Prodical Son returns this Christmas day!
25. December 2007 @ 08:10
HEY ALL!!! MERRY CHRISTMAS TO ALL OF YOU!!!!

I have missed chatting at you all so, so, much, And it has been a heavy burden wearing on my soul that I find it hard to Blog every day like I used to. The medication I'm onm still makes it VERY hard for me to focus and type – it even makes it diffiuclt to dictate to someone else, becase you tend to forget where you pointt was going.

Anway what better day that the birthday of our Lord Jesus Christ could I pick to try my weary hand at Blogging once again?
And know this...even thouhg I have not been posting for the last few months, i HAVE been reading and your comments are simply....glorious, uplifting and so much more than mere words can describe. THey have definately been a source of fuel and lova

for me cna ny family and a lot of other folks out there and for that again I can only say thank-you.

Come to think of it, I find it amazing what my little Blog has turned into this past year and I'm sure it will metaphorphasize again into other even more positive things.

Well, the kids will be getting up soon and thianks to tje generousity of SO many people-, there are so may gifts undeer the tree for my two womderful kids, that it has just simply made me sit here and weep – because months earlier I didn't know how we would even be able to "Do" Christmas this year. And once again, just when you think all is lost, manna appears from heaven in the form of presents for my two amazing little kids. Thanks you Lord!!!!!!! And thank you to all of you who have given so generouersouly and selflessly of yourselves to us this season – we could NOT have done it wothout you this year.
OOPS. I think I hear little feet starting to stir – I better run. We love you all!
So Marryy Christmas to all of you, spelling mistakes and all ☺
Till the next time (which will be soon...I promise)
I lova each and every one of you,
Ken
The Medical Mystery that is Me :) | Comments (56)

Another Day!
Posted by Marilyn
30. December 2007 @ 08:23

Yesterday, Marjorie took Darriane and Sue out to a play in Niagara Falls for a Christmas gift to Darriane. John hung around at

Kenny's (in case). Jerry and I stopped in for a little while to say Hello to Kenny. He was sleeping when we entered but woke up shortly.

The trip to Hamilton on Friday took so much out of him. He is soooo tired.

Sue said the days and nights blend into one another. Not much difference to either for Kenny. The Children's activities keep Sue tuned into daytime though. Sue needed the outing yesterday. She needed to enjoy and not be the constant caregiver, even for a few short hours. Sue said that just seeing Darriane's excitement at the play made her day.

Braeden was staying at Shirley's for the day and night, which was a big help.

Kenny's legs are still swollen up to the knees.

Sometimes, he is so tired, exhausted that he even needs help walking to the bathroom (luckily that does not happen too often). Kenny finds he is not that hungry and has to force himself to eat something.

Like I said, One day blends into the next, without much change. As this old year leaves us & the new year is around the corner, I continue to ask for your prayers for our brother and the family. thanks
Marilyn

*****DEC 31/07: ADDITION*****

My apologies to everyone for not being more specific in the previous Blog entry about Kenny's visit to Hamilton.

We do have to remember that Kenny had to cancel/postpone 3 appointments previous to this past Thursday. Thursday he was scheduled for an appointment and Kenny could not make that one either. When Sue had called to cancel, she was told that the Dr. would be on holidays from Sat. Dec. 29 for 1 week. Sue could bring Kenny in Dec. 28 OR wait until the new year. Kenny and Sue felt that when the going is good....go for it. Kenny wanted to see the Dr. before she left. The Dr. needed to see him anyway before any changes, so now it is just a phone call in the new year. That might be a good thing. If they had waited until the Dr. returned....who knows how Kenny would be then. Would they have to cancel another appointment? Kenny was feeling really guilty about all the appointments that he had to cancel. Kenny was very specific with the Dr. that the ultimate goal is to remove all the patches and just be on the Meth. Kenny and Sue think very highly of the staff at the cancer clinic, and feel that they are being treated with respect and care.

The Medical Mystery that is Me :) | Comments (30)

CHAPTER 64

Ushering in a New Year
2. January 2008 @ 11:00

Hi all. This is not Ken (unfortunately) and its not even Marilyn. It is Craig Frere here, with just a wee bit of an update from the time we were able to spend with Ken and Sue on New Years Eve. It has been our tradition for the past 5 years or so that our two families spend New Years Eve together ushering in the brand new year. We weren't sure that we were going to be able to keep that tradition going this year but praise God that Ken's pain was pretty much under control and we were able to. What a blessing it was that our kids were able to be with Darriane and Braeden for both that night and on boxing day as well. They hadn't been able to see each other for a number of months and they were really glad to be able to have a great time together.

As I said, Ken's pain was level was fairly good that day but he was very tired. He spends a lot of time sleeping these days. I know that he appreciates the visits that he has with friends and family even though it takes a lot out of him. It was good also for Kim and Sue to be together. Ken and I would hear them giggling away in the kitchen about who knows what and we would take a break from watching TV downstairs, look at each other and just shake our heads. While it wasn't as effervescent a party as other years, it was so very good to be there to witness the dawn of another new year.

There is no question that 2007 has been a difficult year but despite that, Ken has not lost his hope for the future. He expressed a couple of different times his hope that 2008 has good things in store. None of us knows for sure what this new year holds for us but it is so important that we never lose hope. Romans 5:2-5 reminds us of this. "And we rejoice in the hope of the glory of God. Not only so, but we also rejoice in our sufferings,   because   we   know   that   suffering   produces perseverance; perseverance, character; and character, hope. And hope does not disappoint us, because God has poured out his love into our hearts by the Holy Spirit, whom he has given us." I can't say that I know what it exactly means to rejoice in my sufferings yet, but I am choosing to stand on the hope that doesn't disappoint.

Happy New Year to you all. I know that if Ken were Blogging here himself, he would remind you that he loves you all and he would wish you much happiness and prosperity this year.

New Day!
7. January 2008 @ 18:07

Well, we all were scared for a day or two. Wondering what had happened to the Blog. Thankfully it is back, & with no help from us. (the computer genius is the one with cancer)

Now for our update:
Kenny is on oxygen now most of the time. That started Sat. Jan. 5 around 4 am. He felt he could not breath well enough on his own. There has been times when he takes it off, but only for a short spell.

He has been trying to eat. Sunday morning he was asking for bacon and eggs. Now he has not really eaten anything in the last few weeks. Sue felt that maybe cream of wheat might be easier on his stomach.

He ate half. (the bowl was not that full) He is having difficulty getting his pills down. He feels that they are getting stuck. He is also unstable on his feet. He fell Sunday afternoon, & he hit his head on the side of the fireplace. That was a major scare for Sue and myself. No bleeding, and nothing was broken. He does have a hard head. ☺

The family has been HANGING out at Kenny and Sue's. Kenny has been wondering why we are always there. Each time he opens his eyes we still seem to be there. "We just like spending time with you and your family" is what we tell him! The family has gone back to work today so his house should have been more quiet.

Please continue to pray for Sue. She needs strength and courage each day.
Thank you for all your prayers, love and comments.
The family has cherished them all.
Marilyn
The Medical Mystery that is Me :) | Comments (61)

CHAPTER 65

John's Two Bits
Re: New Day!
12. January 2008 @ 03:36

"Run with us"
Sung by Lisa Lougheed,
theme song for the cartoon,
Raccoons

When darkness falls,
Leaving shadows in the night,
Don't be afraid,
Wipe that fear from your eyes.

Midnight. It's going to be another long, long night. Marjorie, myself, Marilyn and Jerry are having a "sleepover" (as we told Darriane) this Friday night. Kenny is full of phlegm and has trouble clearing his chest. Both Sue and Marilyn have firm enough voices to get him eventually to respond to drinking water. Marilyn was successful in getting dry eye relief drops into his eyes, one of which was pink from infection and rubbing. Kenny's sleeping now with his mouth open. His chest is so skinny. His bones are like sticks that could easily break. We love him so. Marilyn and Jerry sit quietly "in vigil" on one couch. Marjorie is reading on the other couch. Sue is taking care of the clothes in the drier. Practical things still need doing. It's going to be another long night. Wally and Judy were sent home since we were doing tonight's shift.

Since I started writing these thoughts, I've gone home myself. Marjorie asked me to drive back to Vineland with Jerry and get a good night's sleep. Jerry has a bunch of errands to run tomorrow. Good night's sleep or not, I have to finish these thoughts, whether at Kenny's or here at home. Kenny might be singing with the angels either tonight or tomorrow night. It will be soon. His voice will come back then.

> *The desperate love,*
> *Keeps on driving you wrong,*
> *Don't be afraid,*
> *You're not alone.*

> Chorus
> *You can run with us,*
> *We've got everything you need,*
> *Run with us,*
> *We are free.*
> *Come with us,*
> *I see passion in your eyes,*
> *Run with us.*

Over the past two weeks, Kenny has had the cartoon channel on whenever Marjorie and I visit. I watch these episodes with him.

He and I have similar tastes in cartoons: *The Rocky and Bullwinkle Show, Mr. Peabody's Improbable History, Fractured Fairy Tales, The Flintstones, The Jetsons and The Raccoons.*
We both like Bugs Bunny but can't stand Tweety Bird. Thank goodness for cartoons and the vocal gifts of Mel Blanc, such a great way for Kenny to distract himself from pain. Kenny often

watches cartoons standing up with the aid of his walker, elbows resting on all the pillows he's propped up there. He pays attention to cartoons even when he's doing his walking exercises, what he calls his "Indy 500." My ears always perk up over the lyrics of *The Raccoons* because I like what the message is. In fact, there's always a moral voiced at the end of each episode which takes place in The Evergreen Forest with Bert Raccoon, Cedric and Cyril Sneer.

When the cold wind blows,
Turn your cover to the cold,
Don't be ashamed,
If you need someone to hold.
If you're sinking in quicksand,
And it's dragging you down,
And you feel you're going under,
We'll be around.

Chorus
You can run with us,
We've got everything you need,
Run with us,
We are free.
Come with us,
I see passion in your eyes,
Run with us.

Earlier this evening, Andrew came for a visit. Darriane wanted to go for a walk, just the three of us. She needed things to do as a six year old even though her Daddy was sick. Andrew said no to the walk, he'd come to visit Kenny, so he headed straight downstairs. Darriane and I headed out for our long walk together and dropped in at her friend's, Trinity, a couple of blocks away. Trinity was another six year old attending the other Grade 1 class at the Port

Weller Elementary School. Marjorie and I have elected ourselves
to run distraction or interference, so speak, with the kids.
Entertainment too, I guess. One of us has been doing some special
activity with Darriane lately to take the pressure off Sue's care of
Kenny. Braeden is at Sue's mom's, Shirley's. Thank goodness for
family.

> *And you're behind closed doors,*
> *All alone by yourself,*
> *And you're longing inside,*
> *To be somebody else.*
> *You pick up the telephone,*
> *And there's no one on the line,*
> *Don't be afraid,*
> *'Cause there's still time.*

Kenny's breathing was even for most of the evening when
Marjorie and I had been at the house this Friday evening. Sue was
able to get his Methadone and Atavan into him with Jello
chocolate pudding. He's finding it difficult to swallow pills. He
hardly speaks, less and less than a whisper now. Time is frozen,
everything is slow motion. It takes minutes to get a response, a
nod, a shake of the head, a whisper. What if he finally refuses his
next scheduled meds at 2 or 3 a.m.? What if he goes into a
comma? God, we are still praying for You to intervene, even in the
11th hour. If Kenny dies, what will this do to our faith? I guess real
faith is not Sunday worship but hanging on to God despite sorrow.
Maybe we don't have a choice whatever happens to us. If Kenny
dies, God let him sing again with the angels.

> Chorus
> *You can run with us,*
> *We've got everything you need,*
> *Run with us,*

We are free.
Come with us,
I see passion in your eyes,
Run with us.

If God would have created his miracle, Kenny would already be accepting more food, not less, and we'd know he was improving. He's not. We can only be with him and show him that he is not alone. It's been so sad, so sad for Kenny…and all of us. Earlier in the week, Marjorie and I drove over and it was raining. Marjorie said: "The sky is crying too!" We wanted Kenny to eat something and asked him what he had a hunger for. He wanted "Alphabets". He whispered so low that I couldn't make it out. I thought he had said: "I am pissed" (thinking he was angry). Well, he sure had cause to be with people not hearing him right. I told Sue and Marilyn about my misinterpretation later and they thought it was actually funny. I guess I did too as an afterthought. You must be so frustrated Kenny. I'm so sorry. We can't imagine what all is going through your head with what's happening to you. I'm so sorry.

That sort of thing has happened before more than once when Kenny was not understood. I can think of it particularly when Kenny tried to say something with me and Wally there. Wally is a bit hard of hearing, so I'm supposed to be the "translator." Kenny's question was about when "that girl" (Joanne Hunt) was coming (for touch therapy). I didn't know which girl or what Kenny was talking about? His larynx was shot. It took Sue to put all the pieces together.

I commented that Wally, Kenny and I make up some trio: a guy who couldn't hear, a guy who couldn't talk and a guy who couldn't understand.

All so funny and sad at the same time. I'm so sorry Kenneth.

Thursday night, we held a vigil too. It was the non-working people, Wally, myself and Sue on shift duty. Dad slept on the short couch, his legs tucked under. He commented to me later that he should really cut the arm of the couch off sometime. Sue slept on the other couch (good thing she's short). I slept on the mat on the floor (liking flatness and firmness because of back problems).

So the three of us kept vigil. Ken's Methadone and Atavan were due at 2:30 in the morning. Sue had the awfullest time rousing Ken to awareness. When we finally got him to sit up, his eyes kept rolling back. His mind wanted to fall back to sleep. It took us from 2:30 to 3:45 to get 3 little pills into him. Minutes rolled by without any response. Sue was so great with her voice modulating from gentleness to firmness, waiting patiently at Kenny's non-responsive intervals. Sue herself sometimes has to ask Ken to repeat things because his voice is so very weak. He deliberately did what I considered one of his funny faces by twisting his lips. I said to Sue that he was making a face at her.

Kenny had enough spunk in him to whisper: "That's Bull."

Kenny had to go to the washroom down the hallway twice. Each time Sue walked backwards leading Kenny holding his outstretched arms. Dad walked slowly in behind as "the spotter" in case Kenny should fall backwards.

Kenny was so unsteady in his slow shuffle. He had already fallen and hit his head once on the fireplace earlier that week. Thank goodness for his hard head (and I guess his hard headedness).

Who knows what tomorrow will bring. I'm sure it will take care of itself. This week has been difficult on Ken, on Sue and on Dad, not to mention Marjorie and Marilyn. We have no choice but to plug along in this matter. God knows our sorrow.

> *When darkness falls,*
> *Leaving shadows in the night,*
> *Don't be afraid,*
> *Wipe that fear from your eyes.*

John

CHAPTER 66

Signing Off Book One

Kenny had a hankering for bacon and eggs. I said I'd make them for him, hoping that a bit of food would give him some strength. The smell of frying bacon filled the kitchen and that was soon filled with the smell of scrambled eggs. When was that? Back in November, December?

I put some in a bowl for Kenny and took it downstairs. He only ate a bit and then poked around in the food. He still couldn't keep anything down. It was sad so see. "I'm sorry, Kenny." I wanted to see you eat.

Kenny got weaker and weaker. He was getting less steady on his feet. At one point, he tripped in the family room and crashed his head into the ornamental flashing around the fireplace putting a good dent into the copper framework.

We prayed that God would step in and do something. "Make it stop!" Make the pain stop, make the cancer stop. But it seemed like we were praying into empty space. Kenny was not rallying.

It was my chore to take Darriane out of the house, going for walks with her in the evening, the little 6 year old and myself, to get her out while the adults talked. I'd say, "Let's go visit your cousin,

297

Cody." He lived a couple of blocks away and we'd have snowball fights on the way there. Darriane and I talked about the Christmas lights on the houses or how thick the snowflakes were.

Marjorie and Marilyn took a week off work in mid-January as the family kept vigil for Kenny. There were two couches downstairs: an L shaped one where Kenny lay. Sue curled up on the shorter end of it and then the couch at the back wall where dad sometimes rested. Marjorie and I slept in sleeping bags on the floor. Some family member always accompanied Kenny to the washroom down the hallway when he needed to go in the middle of the night.

Kenny would prop himself onto his walker and one of us would walk behind him with arms stretched out in a large embrace (not touching) but always there in case Kenny teetered over. We'd see him to the bathroom door. He'd manage to close it and once in a while, whoever had walked him to the bathroom, would ask: "Are you alright?" Then the guarded walk would proceed back to his couch and his duvet.

Once, as I recall, Kenny couldn't get to the toilet in time. I offered to clean up the mess but Sue, having nurse's experience, did the chore. It was so hard on Kenny's sisters and on dad, the emotional drain and the pain of seeing Kenny so shrunken by cancer. We kept praying and praying and praying...His body looked withered and just plain worn out. His mind and brain must have been shutting down too. He told Marilyn at one point: "My brain is fucked!"

Some people felt that this next comment should not be mentioned at all to the public. I think it underscores Kenny's humanity and might serve as a reminder that we need compassion as humans.

A day or two before Kenny died, his last words were: "This is crap."

Of course, it was...death and sickness are crap...so is old age and all the slings and arrows of outrageous fortune that mankind is heir to! Kenny was right in uttering these words about how he honestly felt...because he got a raw deal. As a family, we all felt so helpless under the circumstances.

All we could give him in return was our empathy, our feelings of grief and our wishes that the situation was not so.

All we could give him was our time, just being with him, of camping out at his house on the floor in the last days before his death, of attending to his toiletries and of assisting Sue in any way we could with Kenny's meds and comfort on the couch downstairs.

We wished we could have done so much more. Dying is crap! Good for you, Kenny, for uttering just what you thought!

Kenny had trouble swallowing his pills. Sue put them into spoonfuls of pudding and that seemed to go down easier. I remember when Kenny was too weak even to wipe his own nose and actually missed trying to wipe it with a flimsy Kleenex. Family members did that for him. He was becoming more and more helpless.

I tried to write a poem, pleading with God: "If you will not take a prayer/ will you take a tear?" No other words came. No poem. My mind went numb. I felt God was too far away to listen, attending to distant galaxies, too busy planting the seeds of stars to pay attention to our family's needs...but I prayed anyway.

Taking the printouts that Lois from Fair Havens gave us of Kenny's Blog, and making sure it all got retyped into my computer, was emotionally draining. I wished there were more of the printouts, but it was what we had to work with.

How difficult things were, especially the last week and a half. I can (thoroughly) understand why family and friends would not want to revisit a memoir about this, let alone a series of three books in a Trilogy.

I'm going to plug along anyway, now that I've started this journey, one that we were all on with Kenny, "the hardest journey". It's ironic that Kenny's favourite rock group was, "Journey."

It is time to wrap up Book One of *Time in a Bottle Trilogy*. I've divided the books, so that you can quit your reading at this one, and you have the choice not to go on.

Book Two opens with the last few posts in Kenny's Blog where he slips into a coma and dies on January 18th 2008. The Blog soon goes offline after Kenny's funeral.

However, I had more things to say after I discovered Anwar Knight's Blog, the CTV weatherman and how he dealt with his bout of cancer in 2010. There are worthwhile insights there, so many similarities and contrasts with Kenny's struggle.

Book Two also takes a detour back into my own life through the diary I kept at the time and about the murder of Audrey Gleave, my friend in Ancaster, a 73 year old lady who took web design courses at night school through Mohawk College.

My Brother-in-Law
Got Sick

Book Two includes my life as a reporter, why I left the profession, and why I went into teaching instead.

Book Two becomes a story as much about myself, as about Kenny. I hope you choose to read Book Two. I put a lot of work into it.

John Hartig
[brother-in-law]

Acknowledgements

Thanks to my wife, Marjorie, who prefers to remain anonymous and who lets me sneak off at midnight, close the bedroom door, and fire up the computer with a cup of tea by my side, so I can type. Insomnia has its good points.

Thanks to Lois from Fair Havens, whose last name escapes me at the moment, for handing us those pages that she had printed out of *Ken Janzen's Health and Wellness Blog*. They came in handy.

Thanks to Lubomir Cekota, my swimming buddy at the Kiwanis Pool in St. Catharines, for his corrections on grammar and anything to do with history.

Thanks to a former neighbour, Michael Kositsky, for proofreading portions of my first ever attempt at a novel, now turned into a trilogy itself, entitled, *Love and Faith Trilogy* by John Hartig. Michael is a composer of music in various genres.

I'd also like to acknowledge my St. Jerome's High-School teachers, in Kitchener, Ontario, for giving me a good classical education.

First of all, my English teacher, Mr. William Klos, who ignited a love of literature and who read poetry and excerpts with feeling. Also, Mr. Ronald Haston, who made history come alive, especially with his narratives and spirited introductions to every history class. And I must not forget his emphasis on decent research and documentation.

Disclaimer: This is the spot where I wanted to say that Niagara Health Care Services is not the same as it was a decade ago, that it has improved. I cannot say that. It would be a lie.

Just this morning in 2019, I heard about Conservative Premier Doug Ford's announcement that there are more cutbacks coming to our health care system in Ontario.

OHIP, the Ontario Health Insurance Plan, is strapped for cash. Total of 13.5 billion dollars in debt. Doctors want more money. Private companies want more money for their services. The waiting time in the Emergency Ward is 3 to 5 hours. Pay the $45 instead and go by ambulance! The list is getting longer for what the government does not pay. My family physician charges $20 extra out of pocket for a medical note if I need one.

Before my retirement, easily one/third of my paycheque went for taxes, part of which paid for our "free" health care in Canada.

Each new provincial government says that the last government is to blame. That they left them with a huge deficit which they now have to fix. Where do you get the money to balance the budget? Cutbacks of course!

In 1995, Conservative Premier Mike Harris chipped away at Ontario's 11 billion dollar deficit by laying nurses off and installing a useless program called Telehealth Ontario, a 24 hour toll-free help line. Who wants to dial through menus on the phone when you are doubled over in pain? In 1999, Highway 407 was leased for 99 years to a foreign private consortium. Now in 2019, the highway is a lucrative money making proposition but the money is siphoned off to foreign investors. During Harris' tenure, there was also talk of selling off Ontario Hydro and the LCBO [Liquor Control

Board of Ontario] which were also money makers, but the public outrage said no to that.

Things got no better under the Liberals and Premier Dalton McGuinty. The province went into further debt with the cancellation of a huge gas plant deal. A real scandal! Then came a smiling Kathleen Wynne who actually sold off shares of Hydro One and proclaimed that waiting times in hospitals were shorter, when they weren't. Her government never balanced the budget despite getting rid of valuable provincial assets. And now the other party is in again, the Conservatives under Doug Ford, who likes slogans like "a buck a beer" and making "tailgating" legal, where you can drink your own booze in the parking lots for big sports events. Am I hearing right? Are these priorities?

When I had an aneurysm repair in 2017, I came out of the hospital with bed sores. It took 6 months for the open sores in my butt to close up with scar tissue. What was the hospital's excuse? It was the weekend, and there were not enough nurses on staff to turn me over properly.

Whoa! I'm off the track here. This is a rant, not a disclaimer! What was my original point? Oh yes, like my dead brother-in-law, Ken Janzen, might say, "Nothing's changed!"

P.S. There are a bunch of typos and spelling mistakes in Kenny's Blog. When I quoted excerpts from his Blog, I deliberately kept those mistakes in, not because Kenny couldn't spell but because his mind was fogged from his heavy pain killers. Kenny was an excellent writer and computer guy.

Biography

John Hartig is an up and coming Canadian novelist. He's always been a writer, except when he couldn't speak English. He came to Canada with his parents from Austria in 1954 at the age of 8. The threat of being beaten up by his classmates forced him to learn English...very quickly. Soon he had no accent, and soon he was playing outdoor hockey with the gang, and on weekends reading The Last of the Mohicans.

He started writing poetry in high-school. John acquired a Double-Honours B.A. in English and History from the University of Waterloo, then an M.A. in English from McMaster University. His first job as a writer came at the Chilliwack Progress newspaper in British Columbia. He became an editor at Grande Prairie This Week in Alberta.

John left the writing business for a while because the byline did not pay for gas, rent and food. He became a high-school teacher since he already had a Teacher's degree from the University of British Columbia. In later years, he acquired a degree in Corporate

Communications from Sheridan College in the year 2000. Then a
Webmaster Certificate from Mohawk College in the year 2007.
Since he had photography experience from the newspaper trade,
he became a wedding photographer, and a scenery photographer.
It was scenery photography which prompted him to become a
more active Web Designer so he could share his pretty pictures on
the internet.

Now during retirement, John keeps himself busy as an author,
writing novels, specifically murder mysteries. There are always
new frontiers to conquer.

*****

**You can access other John Hartig short stories, novels and poems
through his personal website:**

Website:
www.johnhartig.ca

E-mail:
johnehartig[at]gmail[period]com

Made in the USA
Monee, IL
22 November 2022

17881628R00184